CHURCHILL
THE WRITER

CHURCHILL THE WRITER

His Life as a Man of Letters

KEITH ALLDRITT

HUTCHINSON
LONDON

For Joan
with love
as always

First published in Great Britain in 1992 by
Hutchinson

Random Century Group Ltd
20 Vauxhall Bridge Road, London SW1V 2SA

Random Century Australia (Pty) Ltd
20 Alfred Street, Milsons Point, Sydney, NSW 2061, Australia

Random Century New Zealand Ltd
PO Box 40–086, Glenfield, Auckland 10, New Zealand

Random Century South Africa (Pty) Ltd
PO Box 337, Bergvlei, 2012, South Africa

A catalogue record for this book is available from
the British Library

ISBN 0 09 177085 8

Set in Sabon by Raven Typesetters, Ellesmere Port
Printed and bound in Great Britain by
Mackays of Chatham PLC, Chatham, Kent

Contents

Acknowledgements

In writing this account of Churchill I have been helped by a number of people. I am most indebted to my wife Joan Hardwick who assisted me at every stage of the research and writing, and who took time from work on her own current book to type the manuscript from my nearly illegible handwriting. I must also thank my daughter Miranda for her very willing research help which included some, to me, quite astonishing computer wizardry. My son Benjamin, who is very knowledgeable about Churchill and his time, also made many contributions to the book. To Keith Brace, the Literary Editor of the *Birmingham Post*, I am very grateful for keeping me up to date on books about Churchill.

I should like to acknowledge the work of my predecessors in this particular subject, Martin Weidhorn and Isaiah Berlin. And like anyone who writes about Churchill and his era I am immensely indebted to the prodigious scholarship of Martin Gilbert. I have also been helped by the very innovative work on Churchill by Robert Rhodes James. My very first introduction to Churchill's writings I owe to my aunt, Clare Alldritt Evans.

I thank also the staff of the London Library, the Library of the City of Lichfield and the Reference Library of the City of Birmingham, who helped with the illustrations. In seeing the book through the press, I have depended a great deal on Julian Shuckburgh and on the efficiency and kindness of Mary Scott.

KA

Preface

This biographical account of Winston Churchill focuses on one of the several enterprises that made up his long and complex career. Talking to people about Churchill today, nearly thirty years after his death, I find that there is a tendency to lose sight of the very various, often contradictory, human being that he was. The simple icon of him in Parliament Square expresses a familiar view; it shows his courage, determination and personal force. Certainly these characteristics were a part of his genius but there was also a great deal more to him than these. His very vital intelligence was multi-faceted; it was political and rhetorical, military and administrative, geographical and historical, aesthetic and literary. This last facet as it shows itself in a professional writing career of some sixty years is what I describe here.

Churchill's immense political force has inevitably overshadowed his literary reputation. And received notions of his writing can also be off-putting. As a writer he is often remembered for Churchillese, a grand but pretentious language made up of ringing phrases and sentences that at times have little relationship with the known realities of experience. When, towards the end of his life, his war memoirs and the several volumes of his *History of the English-Speaking Peoples* were appearing, reviewers, however respectful, felt obliged to comment on their wordiness, their dated and artificial rhetoric and the emptiness of many of their histrionic, abstract statements. Churchill the statesman, it was intimated, must always command recognition; Churchill the writer was far less compelling. At his most characteristic he could be turgid; at his worst he could be little more than a windbag.

In the following account of Churchill's literary career I have not sought to ignore these criticisms or to deny that as a writer of English prose his work is uneven. His reputation as an author has been unduly affected by his last books, in which he was most likely to become verbose. Like one of his literary admirations, Samuel Johnson, his image in literary as in political terms can become, restrictingly, that of the last years of his life, the years of the historic wartime Prime Minister and the subsequent memoirist and historian. But there is also the Churchill who wrote prose of an outstanding literary quality which belongs unquestionably in the canon of English literature in this century. It is a prose marked by wit, subtle human insights, pace, drama and a poetic richness and allusiveness. The evolution of this prose style beginning in the last years of Queen Victoria's reign is the prime focus of this account of Churchill's life. It traces his successive achievements as journalist, novelist, essayist, historian, prose miniaturist and biographer.

I have not attempted to relate Churchill's distinguished career as an orator because that would mean a much larger and more diffuse book than I have sought to write. This book is about his long relationship with the reading public rather than with political audiences. What I offer is the story and an assessment of the career of a professional writer which lasted some sixty years and which predated and facilitated his other career in politics. The two careers stand in a creative, dialectical relationship with each other. And it is a loss in our understanding of recent times if the near legendary achievements of the politician and statesman obscure the accomplishments of the man of letters. Churchill's name was one of the twentieth century's additions to that list of writers whose works constitute English literature.

CHAPTER ONE

The Young Journalist

I

Winston Churchill's preparation for a career as a writer can be seen to begin in the summer of 1895 when he was twenty years old. There were two other important events in his life that year. In January his father, Lord Randolph Churchill, died of syphilis after a period of great suffering and social and political humiliation. And in February Winston, who had passed out from Sandhurst a few weeks before, received his commission and began his career as a junior cavalry officer with the 4th Hussars at Aldershot.

Lord Randolph Churchill had a profound influence on his son's life generally, and especially on his literary development. Lord Randolph was one of the most spectacular orators and politicians of late-Victorian England. At the age of twenty-five he was elected to Parliament as member for Woodstock, the Oxfordshire constituency containing Blenheim Palace, the home of his father the seventh Duke of Marlborough. In the early 1880s, when the Liberals were in power under Gladstone, young Randolph and his friends offered a far more vital and compelling critique of the government than that provided by the official Conservative leadership in the House of Commons. Randolph was a very powerful speaker with a Byronic lordliness, impudence and wit. He and his associates came to be recognised as the Fourth Party. They argued for a Conservatism that stood between the die-hards of their own party and the Liberals; they urged that 'Tory

Democracy' which was to be the political philosophy of the young Winston Churchill when, in the late nineties, he first contemplated standing for parliament.

Such was Randolph's hold over the party that when the Conservatives were returned to power in 1886, the new Prime Minister, Lord Salisbury, had, very, very reluctantly, to offer to his comparatively youthful and extremely flamboyant colleague the senior cabinet positions of Chancellor of the Exchequer and Leader of the House of Commons. To great public surprise Lord Randolph's tenure of these two high offices lasted only six months. He could not tolerate the insistent demands for money made upon the Treasury by the Admiralty and the War Office and he submitted his resignation. To his intense disappointment he was never invited to re-enter the Cabinet. What had promised to be an outstanding political career was suddenly ended.

The last nine years of Lord Randolph's life were anticlimactic. Before his illness took hold of him, he continued to indulge his life-long interest in horse racing. And to try to stabilise his always precarious financial position he set off, in 1891, to South Africa in order to write articles on that politically turbulent country for a newspaper, the *Daily Graphic*, which paid him two thousand guineas for twenty articles. Four years later the twenty-year-old Winston Churchill would set off to report on a revolutionary in Cuba for the same newspaper, though not for such good pay. These Cuban dispatches done for his father's former employer were Winston Churchill's first publications except for a few contributions to the school magazine at Harrow.

From his father Winston inherited not just his first publisher but, more importantly, an almost painfully sensitive concern with the fine points of English prose style. Lord Randolph could be an extremely harsh critic of the stylistic qualities of the letters his son wrote to him. When Winston was nineteen and an officer cadet at Sandhurst, his father actually returned one of his son's letters, accompanying it with a letter of his own which is a devastating piece of detailed literary criticism. Lord Randolph concludes, 'This is a letter which I shall not keep but return to you that you may from time to time review its pedantic & overgrown schoolboy style.'

In a letter written from Sandhurst the young cadet comments to his mother on his father's criticisms. His letter broaches the issue of formal as opposed to informal language, the colloquial as opposed to what later in the century will be thought of as 'Churchillian'. He writes, in some frustration, 'I am awfully sorry that Papa does not approve of my letters. I take a great deal of pains over them & often rewrite entire pages. If I write a descriptive account of my life here, I receive a hint from you that my style is too sententious and stilted. If on the other hand I write a plain and excessively simple letter – it is put down as slovenly. I never can do anything right.'

Yet his father's biting criticisms of his style are clearly among the important early influences that made the young Churchill so self-conscious about his use of language. And there can be no doubt about the force of Lord Randolph's own English on his son's literary development. During those months of intense unhappiness which followed on his father's ugly, terrible death and which often brought John Bunyan into his mind, Winston tells his mother, 'From this "slough of Despond" I try to raise myself by reading & re-reading Papa's speeches – many of which I almost know by heart . . .' And these same speeches quickened his interest in the writer who more than any other would influence his style at the outset of his career, his father's favourite author and stylistic model, the eighteenth-century historian and autobiographer Edward Gibbon.

Up to the time of his father's death, his mother's influence on Winston's literary development was slight. But thereafter it was immense. In the late nineties she served as her son's literary adviser, his promoter, the purchaser of the books with which he set out to educate himself, and also, at times, as his literary agent. Before her husband's death in 1895 Lady Randolph, the former Jenny Jerome of New York City, had been preoccupied with her own interests. The daughter of Leonard Jerome, an extremely wealthy Wall Street investor who loved horses, yachts, opera and operatic sopranos (the natural daughter of one of his many liaisons, Minnie Hawk, was to be the first to sing Bizet's *Carmen*), Jenny was very beautiful and very sensuous. She was always dressed in the height of fashion and greatly enjoyed the social activities of the English aristocracy into which she had married; she was avid for the hunting, the horse racing, the week-ending, the flirtations, the dinners and the balls. As her husband's venereal illness developed, she gave herself over to a succession of love affairs including one with the Prince of Wales, the future King Edward VII, and one with Count Kinsky, a young and strikingly handsome Austrian diplomat who was a prominent socialite in the London of that time. Like Jenny herself he was an accomplished pianist; he was also a writer on international affairs and a famous horseman and a winner of the Grand National.

With such involvements Jenny had little time for her two sons, Winston and Jack. Winston's letters from his two preparatory schools and from Harrow are full of urgent pleas that she come and visit him or attend a school function, requests which are usually denied, sometimes at the very last minute. But in the first weeks and months of her widowhood the forty-year-old Jenny took a new interest in Winston and his young brother Jack. 'Remember I only have you & Jack to love me,' she wrote to him in the October of that year of bereavement. She had left London for Paris in order to be freed from the demands of the long period of mourning customarily observed in upper-class England at that time. In Paris she met and had an affair with Bourke Cockran, a prominent New York lawyer and Tammany Hall politician. Cockran was a skilled orator and on meeting Winston was greatly impressed by the young man's abilities with language. Cockran commended his 'lucid and attractive expression' and told him, 'I was so profoundly impressed with the vigour of your language and the breadth of your views.' Churchill was pleased by the admiration shown him by his mother's lover. And Cockran was to continue as an important mentor to Churchill the emerging writer.

To his mother in the August of that same year Winston wrote an important letter in which he tells her of his resolution to obtain for himself a literary education. The letter describes a moment of vocation. The young cavalry officer who both at prep school and at public school had had very little academic ambition or success now announces his determination to be his own teacher. He tells her, 'You see – all my life – I have had a purely technical education. Harrow, Sandhurst – were all devoted to studies of which the highest aim was to pass some approaching Examinations. As a result my mind has never received that polish which for instance Oxford or Cambridge gives. At these places one studies questions and sciences with a rather higher object than practical utility. One receives in fact a liberal education.' Rejecting a rather dull technical book that she has recommended he read, he declares forcefully, 'No – my dearest Mamma – I think something more literary and less material would be the sort of mental medicine I need.' He is, he tells her, already reading a book on political economy and the next step in his career as an autodidact will be a reading of his father's favourite work, the long and voluminous *Decline and Fall of the Roman Empire* by Edward Gibbon.

In the event, Churchill's reading of this great prose work had to be postponed. Shortly after announcing his programme of reading to his mother he seized the opportunity, which she had made for him, to go and observe the revolution going on in Cuba and to send reports to the *Daily Graphic*. Churchill travelled to Cuba by way of New York City, where he stayed with Bourke Cockran in his lavish apartment. Cockran had returned from Paris after ending his affair with Jenny. He would always retain a very kindly attitude to her and to Winston and after his return to London from Cuba, Churchill sent this celebrated orator of the Democratic Party two volumes of Lord Randolph's speeches.

In September of 1896 the 4th Hussars were ordered to set sail for India. Given the good reception of his articles for the *Daily Graphic*, Churchill was reluctant to go. He would have preferred to continue his writing career in England or to be sent to some part of the Empire where war was going on and where he could enjoy 'adventure and excitement', perhaps win a medal and certainly do more journalism. One hope was to go to South Africa, from where his father had sent articles. As so often in the next few years he expected his mother to exploit her many highly placed connections to help him get his way. 'I cannot believe that with all the influential friends you possess and all those who would do something for me for my father's sake – that I could not be allowed to go – were those influences properly exerted.' On this occasion, but not on every other, Lady Randolph failed to pull strings and Churchill had to leave with his regiment for Bangalore in South India. It was here that he resolutely set about working through that hefty syllabus of reading which he had earlier started drawing up for himself.

During Churchill's period of service under the Raj, life for a British officer could be extremely comfortable, if not somnolent. In his autobiography Churchill later remembered the easy life. Officers would be roused and shaved by their Indian servants before breakfasting in the mess. There would be a brief parade and then, as the heat intensified, a return to the mess for lunch followed by a sleep until five o'clock. In the evening Churchill's favourite game, polo, would be played. After ten or twelve chukkahs the officers would take hot baths and retire for more rest. They would then assemble for dinner where they would enjoy 'the strains of the regimental band and the clinking of well-filled glasses'. 'And so to bed.'

But Churchill determined not to allow himself to be assimilated into this pleasurable but soporific routine; he set aside certain hours of the day to work on the lengthy reading list he had devised in order to educate himself. During his first eight months in India his mother sent out to him, at his request, more than fifty volumes. They included Darwin's *Origin of Species*, Adam Smith's *Wealth of Nations*, *The Republic* of Plato and Macaulay's *History of England* and his *Essays*. These last two works were of especial importance to Churchill. Macaulay would remain a literary reference point for him throughout his life. The essays of the great Whig historian which Churchill remembered best in later years were those on Warren Hastings, Frederick the Great, Clive, John Hampden and Chatham. These trenchant, witty and dramatic biographical pieces, constituting an important and distinctive achievement within the history of the English essay, provided a prose form which Churchill would take up and develop later in life in his *Great Contemporaries*. Also Macaulay's notorious piece of literary demolition work, his spectacularly destructive essay in practical criticism entitled 'Mr Robert Montgomery's Poems', made an especial impression on the young subaltern who as a writer would later develop formidable if subtle powers as a critic of men and outlooks and policies.

Macaulay gave Churchill a new sense of English prose. Macaulay, he noted, 'is easier reading than Gibbon and in quite a different style. Macaulay crisp and forcible, Gibbon stately and impressive. Both are fascinating and show what a fine language English is since it can be pleasing in styles so different.' He clearly enjoyed his reading and had a sense of making progress. 'I find my literary tastes growing day by day . . .' He grew ever more conscious of issues of style. The influence of Gibbon, he realised, could become excessive. For instance, describing his voyage out to India he told his mother, 'The voyage may be made by literature both profitable and agreeable.' Then he struck out this statement, adding, 'what a beastly sentence'. He went on. 'I suppress with difficulty an impulse to become sententious. Gibbon and Macaulay, however much they may improve one's composition of essays or reports, do not lend themselves to letter writing.' And in an article on oratory entitled 'The Scaffolding of Rhetoric', which he set about writing at this time, he maintains that the first principle of 'Correctness of Diction' (which he claims to be the first principle of oratory) is the employment of simple vocabulary. 'All the speeches of great English rhetoricians . . . display an uniform preference for short, homely words of common usage – so long as such words can fully express their thoughts and feelings.' Yet at the same time he was still drawn to the Gibbonian manner. He defends himself against his younger brother Jack's criticism of his writing, saying, 'I am sorry you do not appreciate or approve of my literary style. Gibbon in his autobiography says "The habits of correct writing may produce without labour or design the appearance of art and study". That excuse is good enough for me & I hope you will graciously accept it.' He goes on to identify a deterioration in late-nineteenth-century English prose style due to the advances in communications. 'In England, you can in a few hours get an answer to a letter from any part of the country. Hence letter writing becomes short, curt & if I may coin a word "telegrammatic".' He contrasts such writing with that of an earlier age, with that, for instance, of their grandmother the Duchess of Marlborough. 'A hundred years ago letter writing was an art. The Duchess . . . writes a letter far better than most people nowadays. In those times pains were taken, to avoid slang, to write good English, to spell well and cultivate style . . .'

During the early months of 1897 in India the 22-year-old Winston worked away at his reading and at his essay on rhetoric. But as his three months of summer leave grew closer he became anxious to have a break from his self-imposed literary studies and from the boredom of his remote posting in South India. As always this vital, energetic, pushy young man wanted adventure and excitement, and the chance of money and fame, and the journalistic possibilities which, he grew ever more convinced, were his best route to these. That year there was a war going on between the Greeks and the Turks and Churchill made up his mind to go to it as a war correspondent. His plan was to sail from Bombay to Brindisi in Italy and thence to Greece. Yet again the son of a famous father wrote to his glamorous socialite mother demanding that she use her influence to obtain for him a journalist's credentials. The tone he takes towards her is quite brusque. 'I should expect to be paid £10 or £15 an article . . . Lord Rothschild would be the person to arrange this for me as he knows everyone . . . These arrangements I leave to you and I hope when I arrive at Brindisi I shall find the whole thing cut and dried.'

Many years later Churchill was to remark on the way in which, after his father's death, his mother became to him more like a sister. This new mode of relationship starts to show itself in these sentences. It was to be further confirmed when in 1900 Jenny, who was just twenty years older than her son, married Captain George Cornwallis-West who was the same age as Winston.

Unfortunately the war between Greece and Turkey was over by the time Churchill's boat docked at Brindisi. He journeyed on to London, where he indulged in many of the pleasures of that year's London Season. One of the highlights was the Duchess of Devonshire's fancy-dress ball at Devonshire House in Piccadilly. Winston and his brother Jack appeared as attendants on their mother, who went attired as the Empress Theodora, the sixth-century Byzantine empress who had been a courtesan before being wooed and married by the emperor.

That Season was suddenly interrupted by the news of an uprising of Islamic tribesmen on the northwestern frontier of India. It presented just the kind of opportunity that Churchill had been looking for. Through some of his aristocratic connections he had a contact with the general commanding the three brigades that were being sent to suppress the revolt. Instantly Churchill set off for India with every hope of being attached by this general to the British expeditionary force. On arriving in India he was bitterly disappointed to find no offer of a military appointment awaiting him. The only way for him to go to the front, initially, was as a press correspondent. So once again Jenny was dragooned into obtaining a newspaper affiliation for him. She succeeded in making an arrangement for him with Edward Levy Lawson, the proprietor of the *Daily Telegraph*, though for less pay than Winston had asked for. Churchill also managed to get himself appointed as correspondent for *The Pioneer*, a newspaper published in the Indian city of Allahabad and in which the imperialist writer Rudyard Kipling, whom Churchill greatly admired, had published some of his earlier work.

So, granted leave from the 4th Hussars still stationed in the south of India, Churchill now set off for the north of the country. It was to prove to be one of the many important journeys in his life as a writer. The year was 1897. It was the year of Queen Victoria's Diamond Jubilee and the high point in the history of British Imperialism. A year later the composer of *Pomp and Circumstance*, Edward Elgar, would hold the first performance of his *Enigma Variations*, expressing some of the melancholy that marked the nineties. A year earlier there had appeared A.E. Housman's *A Shropshire Lad* and also the first edition of the first popular newspaper, the *Daily Mail*, which would force the *Daily Telegraph* for which Churchill was now writing to appeal to a more middle-class readership.

Churchill went to the northwest frontier as a journalist. But out of his experiences there he produced something that was far more than journalism. At the age of twenty-three he wrote his first book, *The Malakand Field Force*, a work which was to change the course of his life.

II

Churchill's first book proved to be a great success. It received some excellent reviews, brought in royalties the size of which astonished him and led to one of the book's admirers, the Prime Minister, Lord Salisbury, inviting the 23-year-old author to a private interview for the purpose of gaining more information about conditions on the northwestern frontier of India. At his very first attempt Churchill had succeeded in making a name for himself as a writer. It was to be several years before he became at all known as a politician. And clearly the early literary reputation assisted the later political one.

Almost a century after its publication *The Malakand Field Force* is still a very readable book. Though its subject is, to us, a remote, abstruse occasion in political and military history, the vitality of the writing still interests and involves the reader in the story. In his first book Churchill shows himself to have a remarkable literary gift.

Admittedly his style of writing about warfare is markedly different from that to which we have become accustomed in the last eighty years or so. The literary treatment of the subject of warfare was profoundly affected by the recourse to the image, to the specific visual detail which was such an important part of the revolution both in poetry and prose that started in the decade of the 1910s. The great writers on war of this time and after, Wilfred Owen, Isaac Rosenberg, David Jones and Keith Douglas, all present their subject in terms of concrete particulars; Churchill in *The Malakand Field Force* adheres to the verbal procedures of an earlier time in using abstract nouns and factual generalising sentences that do not directly affect the reader's senses and feeling. Here, for instance, is his description of a dramatic occasion on which the British troops retreat before the attacking mountain tribesmen and try to take their wounded with them:

> Several of the wounded were dropped. The subadar major stuck to Lieutenant Cassells, and it is to him that the lieutenant owes his life. The men carrying the other officer, dropped him and fled. The body sprawled upon the ground. A tall man in dirty white linen pounced upon it with curved sword. It was a horrible sight.

To recall, say, Wilfred Owen's poem *Dulce Et Decorum Est* and its presentation of the horrible and to compare it with Churchill's sentences is to see the difference between two conventions in writing. Owen nowhere uses a summarising-and-dismissing comment such as 'It was a horrible sight,' though such a sight is the subject of his poem. Rather he looks more closely into the horror, giving us its actuality in all its terrible visual and palpable detail.

On a few occasions Churchill does write more graphically. This is his description of the removal of the dead from one of the battlefields:

> Riding back I observed a gruesome sight. At the head of the column of doolies and stretchers, were the bodies of the killed, each tied with cords upon a mule. Their heads dangled on one side and their legs on the other. The long black hair of the Sikhs, which streamed down to the ground, was draggled with dust and blood, imparted a hideous aspect to the figures. There was no other way, however, and it was better than leaving their remains to be insulted, and defiled by the savages, with whom we were fighting.[1]

Such visually particularised writing is, however, rare; for the most part the description of this frontier war is factual and dispassionate. It

[1] *The Malakand Field Force* is notorious for its errors in typography and punctuation. I have not corrected any of them in the passages I have cited.

is the language of dispatches. This style of English is one which would have been well known to a young officer. In fact he prints as an appendix to the book a series of dispatches sent by different commanding officers involved in the campaign. When the book was first published these dispatches and the dispatch style of much of the book would doubtless have added to its interest. For *The Malakand Field Force* was in one important respect a work of fast journalism, one that was rapidly written and published, and which dealt with a highly topical subject. But for the reader of today this mode of war description is not what gives the book its interest. What here engages the modern reader and what prefigures the best of Churchill's subsequent books are the pace, the philosophical reflections and the humour.

Pace is an important part of any literary talent and here at the outset of his career as a writer Churchill shows himself to have a sure feeling for it. The sentences, the paragraphing, the sequence of chapters, the unfolding overall design move along methodically and decorously. The first chapter of the book offers a clear evocation of the Himalayan landscape in which the events will take place. Then comes a description of the mountain tribesmen and their religious motives for attacking the British. A chapter is devoted to the outbreak of the revolt. And then each of the following chapters deals, one by one, with each of the British retaliatory and punitive expeditions against the Pathans. The narrative moves along systematically and with due and firm deliberation. The first seven chapters are based on research and hearsay; they deal with events and battles that took place before the young author joined the field force. The descriptions of the war in the subsequent chapters are from his own experience and point of view – though, given the dispassionate and impersonal style of the descriptive writing, this change makes no great discrepancy in the literary character of the book.

The stately pace of the work is disrupted in the penultimate chapter when the writer, having completed his narrative of the campaign, offers a set of suggestions for improving combat procedures. But after this rather disorganised miscellany of proposals, the book, in its final chapter, resumes its measured, purposeful tread and concludes with a rhetorical justification of the presence of the British in India, a presence which is due, so runs the final sentence, to 'the influence of that mysterious Power, which directing the progress of our species, and regulating the rise and fall of empires, has found a needed opportunity for a people, of whom at least it may be said that they have added to the happiness, the learning and the liberties of mankind'.

As these words and many others show, Churchill's account of this episode of imperial experience is by one who is a completely unhesitant, unselfquestioning imperialist. The passages of thought and reflection in the book (and there are a good many of them) are all governed by the assumption that the British represent, and bring with them, civilisation and that the Pathan tribesmen, though very brave, are barbarians. They 'reveal a state of mental development at which civilisation hardly knows whether to laugh or weep'. Their spiritual leaders, the 'Mullahs' and 'Fakirs', elicit the young Churchill's distaste. 'Of some of their manners and morals it is impossible to write. As Macaulay has said of Wycherley's plays, "they are protected against the critics as a skunk is protected against the hunters". They are safe, because too filthy to handle, and too noisome even to approach.' Towards the end of the book the author does appear to have a qualm about the unremitting disgust he feels for the life and culture of the native peoples of the frontier. He describes how, after a battle, the British buried the bodies of the dead which the tribesmen, on capturing the burial ground, dug up and mutilated. In a footnote Churchill gives an explanation for mentioning the matter: 'I draw the reader's attention to this unpleasant subject only to justify what I have said in an earlier chapter of the degradation of mind in which the savages of the mountains are sunk.' This insistent contrasting of the civilised and the savage would, of course, be confirmed by Churchill's deep knowledge of Gibbon's *Decline and Fall of the Roman Empire*, in which the two contrasting adjectives 'Roman' and 'barbarian' govern the design of the history.

For the rest, as Churchill reflects upon his experiences with the field force, he finds no need to justify or explain. Decked out with epigraphs from Lucretius, Virgil, Shakespeare, Byron, Tennyson and, of course, the contemporary imperialist poet he so admires, Rudyard Kipling, and containing allusions to Burke and Macaulay and Omar Khayam, his chapters all contain passages of a magisterial weightiness and certainty that recall one of his life-long favourite authors, Dr Johnson. The following is typical:

> The philosopher may observe with pity, and the philanthropist deplore with pain, that the attention of so many minds should be directed to the scientific destruction of the human species; but practical people in a business-like age will remember that they live in a world of men – not angels – and regulate their conduct accordingly.

To read this and the many other similar passages of pontificating and to recall that they are the work of a 23-year-old is to sense the young Churchill playing a role, expressing his thoughts through the received verbal orthodoxies of an earlier generation. Certainly his youth is a subject about which he is, very explicitly, uneasy. The author who on the title page presents himself as 'Lieutenant, the 4th Queen's Own Hussars' confesses himself anxious about commenting upon the tactics and decisions of senior officers in the campaign. And as he begins, in the final chapter, to give his explanation of the complex politics that involve the Russian empire and the British empire in the mountain regions bordering Afghanistan (an explanation which those who remember the 1980s will find convincing), his youth leads him again to hesitate. 'There will not be wanting those, who will remind me, that in this matter my opinion finds no support in age or experience.'

Yet despite such uncertainty and the rhetorical flourishes that derive from it, there is already a quality in this first book that will continue in all his best work. It is genuineness. Whatever he writes about in this book is intensely important to him. The genuineness of his interest in the northwest frontier, for instance, he shows quite innocently by remarking, without in any way showing off, on the background reading he has done. He has studied the *Record of Buddhistic Kingdoms* of Fa-Hien (he notes, with scholarly care, 'Translated by James Legge M.A., LL.D,') and his awakened interest in other generals who have fought through the same mountain regions in other times has led him to study the experiences of Alexander the Great in these same Himalayas, as related in Arrian's *History of Alexander's Conquests*. And Churchill's fascination with the details of tactics, logistics and the historical and political context of the campaign is always lively. The overall impression that the book leaves is that of an energetically serious young man deeply thoughtful about all the ramifications of the dramatic experience he is undergoing.

Serious but not solemn. The reader is ready to put up with the pompous, portentous paragraphs because the very next paragraph may be one of humour, wit or well-managed irony. One of the principle butts of Churchill's humour in the book are the priests or mullahs, the promoters of the surge of Islamic fundamentalism which has motived the mountain tribesmen to attack the British. Churchill continually mocks their obscurantism and also their dishonesty. A prominent figure in the early chapters is the priest whom Churchill calls the Mad Mullah and whom he describes in the following terms:

> He sat at his house, and all who came to visit him, brought him a small offering of food or money, in return for which he gave them a little rice. As his stores were continually replenished, he might claim

> to have fed thousands. He asserted that he was invisible at night. Looking into his room, they saw no one. At these things they marvelled. Finally he declared that he would destroy the infidel. He wanted no help. No one should share the honours. The heavens would open and an army would descend. The more he protested he did not want them, the more exceedingly they came. Incidentally he mentioned that they would be invulnerable . . . Even after the fighting – when the tribesmen reeled back from the terrible army they had assailed, leaving a quarter of their number on the field – the faith of the survivors was unshaken. Only those who had doubted had perished, said the Mullah, and displayed a bruise which was, he informed them, the sole effect of a twelve-pound shrapnel shell on his sacred person.

Sometimes the humour is more concise, contained within a single sentence, and having an element of the epigram to express a ready youthful irreverence and contempt. 'In the heart of the wild, and dismal mountain region in which these fierce tribesmen dwell, are the temple and the village of Jarobi, the one a consecrated hovel, the other a fortified slum.' Sometimes the humour takes the form of a complex multi-edged irony, one that comments on the British as well as the fundamentalists, as, for instance, in Churchill's comments on one of the Mohammedan rebels who had been persuaded to think himself invincible.

> One man was found the next morning, whose head had been half blown off, by a discharge of case shot, from one of the mountain guns. He lay within a yard of the muzzle, the muzzle he had believed would be stopped; a victim to that blind credulity and fanaticism, now happily passing away from the earth, under the combined influence of rationalism and machine guns.

For the reader of today the irony, the humour and wit are the most compelling qualities of *The Malakand Field Force*. The dispatch writing about the insurgency and the lists of military engagements, of those killed and wounded can be of no wide interest today. And some of the wisdoms delivered in the philosophical passages seem to have been achieved without much pain or difficulty. But when Churchill amuses the reader, as he so often does in this first book, the reader is at once reassured by the author's honest insight into certain human realities and impressed by the trenchancy and dexterity of the language in which it is expressed. For the modern reader, as for those very first readers who admired it in the last years of the nineteenth century, *The Malakand Field Force* marks the debut of a considerable literary talent quite remarkable in a young man scarcely into his twenties.

III

The process of the publication of *The Malakand Field Force* was problematical and painful for its author. Churchill knew that another officer-journalist, Lord Fincastle, who was the correspondent for *The Times* in the Malakand, was also bringing out a book on the frontier war. Most anxious that his own account should appear first, Churchill instructed his mother not to waste time by sending the proofs all the way to India but to get somebody in London to do them.

Ill-advisedly, he suggested his uncle Moreton Frewen, Jenny's brother-in-law, his only relative with any literary experience, who had published works on the currency. The family nickname for Moreton Frewen was Family Ruin. He ran true to form, for his inept editing and proofreading did very great damage to Churchill's text. When, out in India, he finally received the supposedly corrected proofs, Churchill was deeply depressed. He felt shame, he told his mother,

> shame that such an impertinence should be presented to the public – a type of the careless slapdash spirit of the age and an example of what my father would have called my slovenly shiftless habits . . . All this destroys my pleasure in the book and makes its very sight odious to me . . . I writhed all yesterday afternoon – but today I feel nothing but shame and disappointment . . . as far as Moreton is concerned, I now understand why his life has been a failure in the city and elsewhere . . . If you want to imagine my feelings – read Lord Macaulay's essay on Mr Robert Mongomery's poems. I feel as that wretched man did when he first read it.

But such misery proved to be unnecessary. As we have seen, the reviewers were ready to pardon the numerous misspellings, errors in grammar and other blunders. And soon the aspiring young author was exulting in his success with reviewers and readers. He quickly started to plan the next steps in his career as a writer, declaring, 'Literary excellence is what I aim at,' and announcing his intention 'to write something that will take its place in permanent literature'. He had three writing projects in mind: a biography of Garibaldi, a volume of short stories to be entitled 'The Correspondent of the New York Examiner' and 'A short and dramatic History of the American Civil War'. Some of the short stories which derived from his time with Bourke Cockran in New York City were roughed out and one at least was completed. But Churchill did not proceed with either the biography or the book on the American Civil War. His mind was perhaps too taken up with another war, one that was going on at that very moment, the British campaign to bring the Sudan back under imperial control.

During the early months of 1898 he nagged on at his mother to get her many friends in high places to have him attached to Kitchener's expeditionary force in the Sudan.

> Oh how I wish I could work you up over Egypt! I know you could do it with all your influence – and all the people you know. It is a pushing age and we must shove with the best . . .

He grew obsessed with the idea that it was in the campaign on the Nile that he could best add to his reputation as a journalist and writer and perhaps also win military fame.

> . . . Egypt. Please redouble your efforts in this direction . . . I am determined to go to Egypt and if I cannot get employment or at least sufficient leave, I will not remain in the army. There are other and better things ahead. But the additional campaign will be valuable as an educational experience – agreeable from the point of view of an adventure – and profitable as far as finance goes as I shall write a book about it.

His mother's many efforts on his behalf were slow to have any effect. So when his summer leave came round again he invested in a steamship ticket and set off from India for England, as he had once done before, to see what he could achieve for himself.

His determination was rewarded. He took advantage of his earlier brief contact with the Prime Minister, Lord Salisbury, and wrote to him asking him to use his influence. Within four weeks Churchill was on his way to Cairo. He had been attached to a cavalry regiment, the 21st Lancers, as a supernumerary lieutenant. The *Morning Post* had also agreed to pay him £15 a column for dispatches about the war on the Sudanese Nile. These writings were to be the beginnings of Churchill's second book, *The River War*.

IV

A work of non-fictional prose, *The River War* is an account of the campaign of British and Egyptian forces against another Islamic fundamentalist movement, one that was founded in the Sudan in the early 1880s by Mohammed Ahmed, the religious leader known as the

Mahdi. The movement was continued under the leadership of his successor, the Khalifa. The war was fought in the valley of the River Nile in Sudan in the years 1896–1899. The Anglo-Egyptian triumph was assured by the decisive victory at Omdurman in September 1898. Churchill's book appeared in the following year.

The work has the same basic structure as that of *The Malakand Field Force*. There is first some description of the Nile valley in the Sudan and then some prehistory which explains the reasons for the conflict. Then comes a description of the early experiences of the expeditionary force as it crosses from Egypt into the Sudan. At the beginning of the second volume of what was first published as a two-volume work, the narrative becomes first-hand as Churchill himself, against the wishes of the commander in chief, General Kitchener, joins the task force and participates in what is the climax of its mission, the great battle against the Dervishes for control of their political and religious capital, the city of Omdurman. As in his first book, Churchill concludes with some rather desultory and disjointed comments on the conduct of the war; he also assesses the social and political prospects for the Sudan following the allied victory.[1]

But though very similar in design to its predecessor, *The River War* is, in literary terms, a very much more substantial and considerable work. It is a much longer book that tells a longer story. It has more narrative interest and suspense; it has some of the qualities of epic. It is informed by a great amount of background reading and research. And stylistically it has a new sense of, and a confidence in, its readership, which must have come from the very friendly reception enjoyed by *The Malakand Field Force*.

Churchill delivered the manuscript to Longman's approximately one year after the Battle of Omdurman and his departure from the Sudan. This is a remarkable achievement, for the book involved not merely the writing of some nine hundred pages but also the gathering, as he tells us in his preface, of 'the written evidence of independent, disinterested eyewitnesses'. It also involved a very large amount of research work. Churchill clearly found it necessary to find out for himself and for the reader the historical context of what was, and would always be remembered as, one of the most important experiences of his life, the Battle of Omdurman and his part in the great cavalry charge of the 21st Lancers. During the twelve months of composition he read very widely in the subject and at the beginning of the first volume names twenty-two titles in his List of Principal Works Consulted.

[1] In subsequent editions of the book much of this material was deleted. The sketches by Churchill's fellow-officer, Angus McNeill of the Seaforth Highlanders, were also omitted.

But *The River War* is not made up of a culling and reproducing of pieces of information from other texts. In his use of sources the 24-year-old author shows himself to be a writer of considerable imaginative powers. His method is that of a serious historical novelist; he takes the received evidence and transmutes it so that the reader receives it as experience rather than fact. In reading the first part of the two volumes, which deals with events that occurred prior to Churchill's arrival in the Sudan, it is very easy to forget that the author did not witness what he presents and that what we are reading is an imaginative reconstruction from other literary sources. Here, for instance, is a description of an incident that took place weeks before Churchill joined the expeditionary force. One of the British gunboats is trying to make its way down the Nile against the rifle-fire of the Dervishes on the river bank. The prose is carried along by a relentless pace and by lively similes that convey a sense of the actual, of reportage rather than reconstruction.

> Beyond the flood waters of the river, backed against a sky of staring blue and in the blazing sunlight, the whole of the enemy's position was plainly visible. The long row of shelter trenches was outlined by the white smoke of musketry and dotted with the bright-coloured flags waving defiantly in the wind and with the still brighter flashes of the guns. Behind the entrenchments and among the mud houses and enclosures strong bodies of the *jibba*-clad Arabs were arrayed. Still further back in the plain a large force of cavalry – conspicuous by the gleams of light reflected from their broad-bladed spears – wheeled and manoeuvred. By the Nile all the tops of the palm-trees were crowded with daring riflemen, whose positions were indicated by the smoke-puffs of their rifles or when some tiny black figure fell, like a shot rook, to the ground. In the foreground the gunboats, panting and puffing up the river, surrounded on all sides by spouts and spurts of water, thrown up by the shells and bullets, looked like portly gentlemen pelted by schoolboys. It was however, a more dangerous game. Again the flotilla drew near the narrow channel; again the watching army held their breath; and again they saw the leading boat, the Metemma, turn and run downstream towards safety, pursued by wild cheers of the Arabs.

Churchill is as effective in evoking characters about whom he has read as he is in recreating incidents. He begins his prehistory of the Nile war with the boyhood and youth and early successes of the Mahdi, the Dervish leader and Mohammedan zealot who inspired his people to evict the Egyptians and their British associates from the Sudan in the mid-1880s. His activities were the original cause of the war which was fought to reconquer the Sudan in the late nineties, the war in which Churchill fought. The Mahdi was the original enemy. Yet Churchill presents him without any suggestion of caricature or distortion. His personality and dynamic career are fully described and he is present in the book as a fully understandable human being. There is even some sort of sympathy for him on Churchill's part.

> But, whatever is set to the Mahdi's account, it should not be forgotten that he put life and soul into the heart of his countrymen, and freed his native land of foreigners. The poor miserable natives, eating only a handful of grain, toiling half-naked and without hope, found a new, if terrible, magnificence added to life. Within their humble breasts the spirit of the Mahdi roused the fires of patriotism and religion. Life became filled with thrilling exhilarating terrors. They existed in a new and wonderful world of imagination.

And as he takes leave of this character in his narrative, Churchill dissociates himself from the popular and reductive attitude to the Mahdi among the British and concludes with an admiring rhetorical salute:

> I do not share the popular opinion, and I believe that if in future years prosperity should come to the peoples of the Upper Nile, and learning and happiness follow in its train, then the first Arab historian who should investigate the early annals of that new nation, will not forget, foremost among the heroes of his race, to write the name of Mohammed Ahmed.

Another character who figures in Churchill's lengthy historical preface, and who is portrayed in all his human complexity and contradictions, is General Gordon. In a famous episode in late-Victorian history this very experienced and well-travelled general was sent from London to supervise the evacuation of British and Egyptians at the time the Mahdi's forces took control of the Sudan. On his arrival in Khartoum, Gordon soon found himself besieged by the Dervishes. In giving his own suspenseful account of this long siege, Churchill draws upon Gordon's own *Journals at Khartoum*. On several occasions he quotes from them. But, overall, the story is a thorough reworking of the sources to make for a narrative of almost novel-like interest. He similarly adapts accounts of the capture of the city and of Gordon's murder and mutilation so that these horrific events are conveyed vividly and dramatically. The fate of the General is that much more affecting to the reader because Churchill has made the man so real as he evokes Gordon's courage and capriciousness, his Christian idealism and violent anger.

General Gordon was murdered in 1885, when Winston Churchill was a schoolboy of eleven years of age. And in reading the account of the siege and the ultimate atrocity, one senses that the writing is at times informed by boyhood memories as well as by research reading. Certainly he recalls the bitter national disappointment and humiliation when the rescue expedition sent, belatedly, to save the General arrived a couple of days too late.

> These events produced a profound feeling of despondency in Great Britain. The shame associated with the Soudan [sic] made its name odious to the whole people. The heavy losses in men and money caused all projects for the recovery of the territory to be unpopular. The nation was prepared to accept its humiliation and acquiesce in its defeat . . . Continental observers did not hesitate to declare that this failure was only the beginning of the end. And in a hopeless way the belief was widely shared in England.

Churchill also recalls his father's concern, very early on in the crisis, about the catastrophe threatening Gordon at Khartoum. He remembers and cites the very day on which the first question was asked in the House of Commons, and by Lord Randolph Churchill, about the envoy's safety. His contempt for the Liberal government of the day and its policies of dithering and delay is intense: 'The case against Mr Gladstone's administration is so black that historians will be more likely to exercise their talents in finding explanations and excuses than in urging the indictment.'

Churchill's feeling of personal and familial involvement in the story of the Sudan is again revealed when he suggests that it was his father's political philosophy that helped to regenerate Britain and made possible the British return to the Sudan. For 'in the freshening breeze of Tory Democracy, pride in the past and hope for the future came back to the British people'. One of the emphases contained within the notion of Tory Democracy is what Churchill terms Imperial Democracy, a regenerative idea whose hour, in the late nineties, had come.

> The idea of Imperial Democracy – a great empire ruled under the crown by a greater people – was no longer a philosophical dream . . . men looked towards Egypt and so remembered the lost provinces and the tragedy with which the name 'Khartoum' must, despite all later successes, be for ever associated.

After some two hundred pages of fast moving prehistory, Churchill sets about telling the story of the British return to Khartoum. The episode is surely one of the great feats of British imperialist experience.

And it is a mark of Churchill's power as a writer that we, who have seen the much vaster achievement in daring, engineering and logistics that put human beings on the moon, should be gripped by this step-by-step and highly detailed account of the sending of an army down the Nile at the end of the last century. Much of the story has to do with the battles against the Dervishes in the course of the long journey. But there is much also about the practical difficulties of moving the great army that included camels and gunboats and mules and artillery. One entire chapter is devoted to a description of the building from scratch of more than a hundred miles of desert railway. Such a subject could be drily technical, but Churchill gives us the detailed actuality and the thrill and excitement of a very risky enterprise. This chapter is in fact more colourful and memorable than some of those dealing with the actual warfare.

The word warfare raises a stylistic and thematic issue that lies at the centre of this work on military and imperial adventure. For the modern reader cannot help but ask about this campaign in the Sudan, was it a war or was it a massacre? As we read of battle after battle, skirmish

INTO THE WILDERNESS

Building a railway into the Sudan in the late 1890s. An illustration done by one of Churchill's brother officers for the first edition of The River War.

after skirmish, in which vast numbers of poorly armed Dervishes are mown down by the automatic weaponry of the invaders, we find it difficult to grasp the rightness of Imperial Democracy. This uneasiness is something which is shared by the author himself. Certainly there was a part of the young Churchill that loved fighting and war. The first sight of the Dervish army drawn up before Omdurman was 'the impression of a lifetime: nor do I expect ever again to see such an awe-inspiring or formidable sight'. And as actual combat he recalls it in a prose that pulses with excitement. 'We were "in touch"; and that is a glorious thing to be, since it makes all the features of life wear a bright and vivid flush of excitement, which the pleasures of the chase, of art, of intellect or love can never exceed and merely equal.' But at the same time Churchill finds something appalling in the mowing down of the Arab horsemen by the British artillery and the Maxim guns. 'It was a terrible sight, for as yet they had not hurt us at all, and it seemed an unfair advantage to strike thus cruelly when they could not reply.' The horror of the actuality of the Arab charge against British guns is conveyed with a vividness such as is not be found in *The Malakand Field Force*.

> Eight hundred yards away a ragged line of men was coming on desperately, struggling forward in the face of the pitiless fire – white banners tossing and collapsing; white figures subsiding in dozens to the ground; little white puffs from their rifles, larger white puffs spreading in a row all along their front from the bursting shrapnel. The picture lasted only a moment, but the memory remains for ever.

Churchill is dismayed by the conduct of the British after their final victory. He criticises Kitchener, to whom he is invariably, though perhaps sometimes grudgingly, fair, for ordering the destruction of the Mahdi's tomb and the exhumation and mutilation of the body. 'Such was the chivalry of the conquerors', writes Churchill bitterly, adding, 'No man who holds by the splendid traditions of the old Liberal party, no man who is in sympathy with the aspirations of Progressive Toryism, can consistently consent to such behaviour.'

The ambivalence, the skepticism, the irony of a writer who is a warrior but not a jingo also underlie the structuring of the narrative climax of the second volume and, indeed, of the work as a whole. There are towards the end two contrasting chapters, each of which can stand in its own right as a classic essay about war. The first is entitled 'The Battle of Omdurman' and presents the tactics, the drama, the excitement of a famous battle. The pendent chapter is entitled 'After The Victory' and has as its central passage a description of Churchill's walk upon the battlefield two days after the fall of Omdurman. It is a description of the visual horror of the 7,000 Dervish dead left lying about and of the terrible stench of 'the monstrous dead' who were 'destroyed not conquered by machinery'. There was 'nothing *dulce et decorum* about the Dervish dead', remarks Churchill in a comment that again prefigures Wilfred Owen's famous poem. And as Owen was to seek to shock his complacent reader by detailing some realities of war in his poem, Churchill also threatens us with the appalling. He asks if the reader would like to 'be furthered sickened by the horrors of the battlefield?' And, felinely, he ventures the image of 'a human being partly putrefied but still alive'.

The divided vision which governs the structure of this story of a great adventure extends even to the smallest points of style. It expresses itself in that ironic collocation of noun and adjective which Churchill had learned from Gibbon but which, very early in his writing career, he had begun to develop in his own way. As he reports one occasion of the butchering of the Dervish troops, he speaks unobtrusively, almost parenthetically and yet damningly of 'that mechanical scattering of death which the polite nations of the earth have brought to such monstrous perfection'.

The River War is again one of most striking literary precociousness. As we reflect on fine points of style or the authorial confidence or the range of the scholarship or the dynamic narrative prose, it comes as a shock to remember again that this was the work of someone who was still only twenty-four years old. *The River War* is unquestionably a classic of historical writing. That it could have been written by someone so very young is the evidence of what those about him were beginning to recognise, an outstanding literary giftedness. The success of the book posed a question about his future career. Should he continue as an army officer? Or should he resign his commission and become a full-time writer?

CHAPTER TWO

Novelist and War Correspondent

I

After the capture of Khartoum Churchill returned to London, where he spent most of October and November of 1898 before reluctantly returning to his regiment in South India. As he began his research for *The River War*, he also assisted his mother in a literary venture which she had decided upon. Nearly forty-five years old now, Jenny suddenly tired of the prospect of a further succession of fashionable parties, dinners, race meetings and hunt balls. She wanted something else in her life and she decided to found a literary review. Wishing to make it attractive to readers in both her native land and her adopted one, she called her periodical, against Winston's advice, *The Anglo-Saxon Review*. Her publisher was to be John Lane, who earlier had brought out the most famous literary periodical of the nineties, *The Yellow Book*, in which had appeared the work of Henry James, Max Beerbohm, Oscar Wilde, Arthur Symons and Aubrey Beardsley.

On New Year's Day 1899 Winston wrote to congratulate Jenny on her venture. The very mannered and gallant Gibbonian antitheses do not conceal a certain patronising tone in her 24-year-old son, who was also an important editorial collaborator. Nor do the lordly eighteenth-century compliments hide the simple hope that the new literary review may assist mother and son with one of their abiding problems, money. The young man told his mother,

THE

ANGLO-SAXON

REVIEW

A QUARTERLY MISCELLANY

EDITED BY

LADY RANDOLPH SPENCER CHURCHILL

VOL. I. JUNE 1899

JOHN LANE

LONDON AND NEW YORK

1899

The title page of the periodical founded by Lady Randolph and produced by John Lane who, in the 1890s, had published The Yellow Book.

> You will have an occupation and an interest in life which will make up for all the silly social amusements you will cease to shine in as time goes on and which will give you in the latter part of your life as fine a position in the world of taste & thought as formerly, & now in that of elegance and beauty. It is wise and philosophical. It may also be profitable. If you could make £1,000 a year out of it, I think that would be a little lift in the dark clouds . . .

Always in the letters between Jenny and Winston in these years there is a concern, a worry, even overt argument between them, about money. But on Winston's part there is always an insistence that the periodical should maintain high literary standards as well as being profitable. He fears that Jenny might take the *Review* downmarket and urges that it be 'Literary, artistic, scholarly always – but blood and thunder never'. The *Review* did print material from some of the leading writers of the nineties such as George Bernard Shaw, Swinburne, Andrew Lang, Max Beerbohm, Edmund Gosse, Edward Garnett, George Gissing, Stephen Crane and Henry James. Winston sought out contributions for his mother such as that from Sir Rudolph Slatin, the great expert at that time on the Sudan and one of the sources used in the writing of *The River War*. And he always had an eye for literary quality. His own essay, 'The Scaffolding of Rhetoric', he decided rigorously, was not quite good enough for *The Anglo-Saxon Review*. 'My article on Rhetoric is not good enough for the Magazine. It would do for *Nineteenth Century* – but it is too much to expect it to make its own reputation as well as that of the paper.'

The first volume of *The Anglo-Saxon Review* appeared in June 1899; there would be nine more before publication was ended in the autumn of 1901. Throughout that period Winston constantly encouraged his mother in her venture and she was always anxious to promote him. There can, for instance, be no doubt about who is being referred to in the editorial comments in the fourth edition of the magazine which deal with the war correspondents who have made their names reporting the recent imperial wars. 'One or two men have appeared – one at least who by common consent, deserves to hold the highest place as an observer and recorder of warlike scenes and episodes.'

Just a few months before the first issue of *The Anglo-Saxon Review* appeared, Churchill took a major decision concerning his own future career. He decided to become a full-time professional writer. His expenses in India were more than his salary and his small allowance from his mother could cover. More importantly, he felt that South India was an imperial backwater in which he, who remarked at this

CONTENTS

The Contents page from one edition of Lady Randolph Churchill's The Anglo Saxon Review.

time 'I have nothing else but ambition to cling to', could not let that intense ambition realise itself. But it is evident that his resolution to leave the army and to live by his pen was accompanied by some apprehension. He felt it necessary to write a long letter justifying his action to his grandmother, the Duchess of Marlborough. 'Had the army been a source of income to me instead of a channel of expenditure – I might have felt compelled to stick to it. But I can live cheaper and earn more as a writer, special correspondent or journalist: and this work is moreover more congenial and more likely to assist me in pursuing the larger ends of life.'

An event in Churchill's literary career which shortly preceded, and very probably assisted, this decision was the acceptance of his novel *Savrola* both for magazine serialisation and for publication in book form. This novel had been Churchill's very first attempt at writing a book. But by the time he had completed five chapters, work was interrupted by the joining of the campaign on the Indian northwest frontier and by the writing of *The Malakand Field Force*. A resumption of the work was yet again interrupted by the expedition to the Sudan and the writing of *The River War*. But on his return from that adventure Churchill finally completed his novel.

His mother, employing the services of the A.P. Watt literary agency, sold the serial rights to *Macmillan's Magazine* and the novel came out as a book in the early weeks of 1900, some two and a half years after it had been begun. During the several phases of composition Churchill tried different titles and subtitles. He finally settled for the title *Savrola*.

In later life Churchill disparaged this book. 'I have consistently urged my friends to abstain from reading it,' he once wrote, though at the same time noting, with surely a touch of pride, that it was 'subsequently reprinted in various editions' and 'yielded in all over several years about seven hundred pounds'. For the reader of today *Savrola* is, despite some very obvious limitations, a lively and an interesting read. What is most immediately entertaining is that, as one reviewer put it in 1900, 'it is rapid and thrilling, and crammed with fighting'. The book is a romance that tells the story of how Savrola, the hero and leader of the freedom-loving people of Laurania, finally ousted Antonio Molara, the despotic president who had ruled for five years after suspending popular rights and the democratic constitution. Encouraged by his villainous secretary and adviser, Miguel, the President asks his beautiful wife, Lucile, to become friends with Savrola in order to discover his plans for the revolution which all are expecting. Lucile and Savrola fall in love and Savrola is almost compromised in the eyes of the people by his association with her. But

SAVROLA

By the Rt. Hon.

WINSTON S. CHURCHILL

A Romance thrilling with passion, intrigue and deeds of daring —with a world-shaking revolution for a background.

Now ready, at all Booksellers and Newsagents

SIXPENCE

The Latest addition to

NEWNES' 6d. FAMOUS NOVELS

Post free 8d., from Geo. Newnes, Ltd.

3-12 Southampton St., Strand, London, W.C.

The advertisement for Churchill's philosophical adventure novel, Savrola, *first published in 1900.*

his great oratorical powers save him. He leads the revolutionaries to a great victory, President Molara is killed and Savrola and Lucile are free to marry. Unfortunately, by characteristically sticking to a point of principle, Savrola loses the respect of the revolutionary committee, is betrayed by the dastardly Miguel and has, with Lucile, to flee Laurania and live in exile. In the last couple of paragraphs of the romance, the author, rather abruptly, announces a subsequent change in the political climate in Laurania which allows Savrola and his consort to return there and to live happily ever after.

But the book is a good deal more than just such a fast-paced yarn peopled with what that same early reviewer called 'the stock puppets of brisk romance'. And it is more than subsequent commentators and critics have allowed. Most of the characters are stock types, it is true, but this could not be said of the central character Savrola. For this figure, who concerns the author far, far more than any of the others, has a complexity that gives the book a genuine thematic interest beyond what is indicated by the word romance as a limited, even pejorative, category in fiction. 'You will like the hero,' wrote Churchill to his favourite aunt, Leonie Leslie, in May 1898, 'the Great Democrat, a wild sceptic with an equally powerful imagination.' He also told her in the same letter that the novel 'appeals to all tastes from philosophical to bloodthirsty and is full of wild adventures and atheistic philosophy.'

Some of the philosophical concerns in the book are clearly those of the young Winston Churchill. Most of the books listed in the library of the philosopher-democrat Savrola are the same as those which Churchill had read in his programme of self-education. Bryan Magee once wrote about the identification of the author with the hero Savrola. And it is true that the young Churchill in his presentation of 'the Great Democrat' gives a prescient account of what his own style as a politician and leader will be like. Savrola has the same presence, the same perfunctory way with official papers, the same ability to relax or nap during times of great political crisis, and above all the same great oratorical powers.

Savrola is also in part a portrait of Churchill's father, whose political fate was very much in his thoughts as a long-bereaved young man. Savrola has Lord Randolph's flamboyance and his ability to sway great crowds with his rhetorical powers. (A whole chapter entitled 'The Word of the Magician' is devoted to the careful description of the making of such an arousing, and then finally inflammatory, speech.) As Lord Randolph the Tory Democrat felt himself betrayed by his supporters, so is the Great Democrat of Laurania betrayed by his. And as Lord Randolph held a difficult position between diehard Toryism on the one hand and radicals and revolutionaries on the other, so does Savrola have to resist both a tyrannical president and the Marxist revolutionaries.

These latter are shown by the author to be a very radical lot. They seek not just economic socialism but also a sexual socialism, which greatly perturbs the beautiful heroine Lucile. Here is their leader, Karl Kreutze, speaking of Savrola to one of his fellow-socialists:

> '. . . He is not one of us. He has no sympathy with the cause. What does he care about a community of goods?'
>
> 'For my part,' said the first man with an ugly laugh, 'I have always been more attracted by the idea of a community of wives.'
>
> 'Well that too is part of the great scheme of society.'
>
> 'When you deal them out, Karl, put me down as part proprietor of the President's.'
>
> He chuckled coarsely. Lucile shuddered. Here were the influences behind and beneath the great Democrat of which her husband had spoken.

The element of melodrama in this idea of socialism has its counterpart, though to a lesser extent, in the ideas and thoughts of the hero which are so important a thematic part of the book. 'All my philosophy is put into the mouth of the hero,' Churchill told his mother. And a few months later, in February 1898, he attempted to explain to her some of the difficulties this was causing him: '. . . the novel remains half finished. But there is no hurry about it and as I have put and am trying to develop in the mouth of the hero a cheery but I believe a true philosophy it takes much thought.'

A philosophy that is cheery but true? The cheeriness we can see in the author's style and in Savrola's conduct as man of action. But the 'true philosophy'? One indication of what this is is Churchill's quotation from Schopenhauer in this same letter. For this allusion reminds us of Savrola's scepticism about, even contempt for, the things of this world. Here is a description of his study, concluding with an arresting final clause that shows the philosophic stance:

> A half empty box of cigarettes stood on a small table near a low leathern armchair, and by its side lay a heavy army-revolver against the barrel of which the ashes of many cigarettes had been removed. In the corner of the room stood a small but exquisite Capitoline Venus, the cold chastity of its colour reproaching the allurements of its form. It was the chamber of a philosopher, but of no frigid academic recluse; it was the chamber of a man, a human man, who appreciated all earthly pleasures, appraised them at their proper worth, enjoyed, and despised them.

The world weariness which recurs in Savrola's mind is one of the several qualities which remind us that the novel is a work of the 1890s. It does not, of course, belong with the naturalist fiction that was such an important literary feature of the decade. Such fiction Churchill was keen to repudiate, saying proudly of *Savrola*, 'It is destitute of two elements which are popular in modern fiction – *squalor and animal emotions*.' These two italically emphasised terms refer presumably to works such as George Moore's naturalist novel *Esther Waters*, which appeared in 1894, and to Thomas Hardy's *Tess of the D'Urbervilles* of 1891, and to his last novel (before he abandoned the form in the face of public and critical hostility), *Jude The Obscure* of 1895.[1]

Churchill was clearly a part of that hostility. *Savrola* is completely innocent of any awareness of sexual realities or of contemporary social realities, even though the book is explicitly set in the year 1885. His novel belongs rather with that other major tradition of the nineties

[1] This last novel Churchill read in the late summer of 1897 while on board ship sailing back to India to rejoin his regiment.

exemplified by writers whom we sometimes call aesthetes, sometimes decadents, sometimes symbolists – writers such as W.B. Yeats, Ernest Dowson and Lionel Johnson. This is not to suggest for a moment that Lieutenant Churchill sympathised with any of these poets, but rather that the decade was marked by two distinct sensibilities and that he was to a considerable extent affected by the latter. The novel contains, for instance, a discussion upon the 'Foundation of Beauty' which the author himself considered 'clever and very thoughtful'. And the hero of the novel is not satisfied by common perception. Savrola often quits the world of public life, goes up on to the roof of his house and gazes at the stars, pondering the possibilities of worlds other than this.[1] Here is his *fin-de-siècle* yearning for something beyond everyday reality:

> By a few manipulations the telescope was directed at the beautiful planet of Jupiter, at this time high in the northern sky. The glass was a powerful one, and the great planet, surrounded by his attendant moons, glowed with splendour . . . Long he watched it, becoming each moment more under the power of the spell that star-gazing exercises on curious inquiring humanity.
>
> At last he rose, his mind still far away from earth. Molara, Moret, the party, the exciting scenes of the day, all seemed misty and unreal; another world, a world more beautiful, a world of boundless possibilities enthralled his imagination.

Along with this special nineties propensity for escapism, for retreat into the magical and the beautiful, the philosopher Savrola, like so many others in the decade, is troubled by eschatological possibilities.[2] (Even a good part of his first private conversation with Lucile is devoted to this topic.) The passage above continues:

> He thought of the future of Jupiter, of the incomprehensible periods of time that would elapse before the cooling process would render life possible on its surface, of the slow steady march of evolution, merciless, inexorable. How far would it carry it them, the unborn inhabitants of an embryo world? Perhaps only to some vague distortion of the vital essence; perhaps farther than he could dream of . . . And then fancy, overleaping space and time, carried the story to periods still more remote. The cooling process would continue; the perfect development of life would end in death; the whole solar

[1] One wonders if these passages are in any way indebted to another novel of Thomas Hardy's, *Two On A Tower*.

[2] A fashionable sadness, melancholy and world weariness inform Churchill's remark in 1897 that 'I have worked into the hero's part a good deal of that sad cynical evolutionary philosophy which is so characteristic of modern thought and which claims a good deal of my sympathy.'

> system, the whole universe itself, would one day be cold and lifeless as a burned out firework.
>
> It was a mournful conclusion. He locked up the observatory and descended the stairs, hoping that his dreams would contradict his thoughts.

The insistence in this and many other passages upon the dream as a release from the melancholy prospect of the cosmos and its dynamics is all very much of the time. So too is Churchill's suggestion that Savrola is something of a superman. In this respect he is often reminiscent of another literary creation of the 1890s, Sherlock Holmes. He is to those around him and his followers as Holmes is to Watson. At a moment of crisis, writes Churchill, there was a 'turning instinctively to the greater soul and the stronger mind'. We are told that 'his great soul was above the suspicion of presumption'. Savrola, like Holmes, also uses narcotics to heighten and energise his consciousness. At the climax of the novel we read:

> He went to a little cabinet in the corner of the room and poured himself out a patent drug, something that would dispense with sleep and give him fresh energy and endurance.

And like Holmes he is the mastermind. The revolution he understands and organises and manages down to the tiniest detail: 'Nothing had been forgotten by that comprehensive mind.' Savrola also has Holmes's clinical detachment. When the revolution first starts, one of his followers, Moret, is convulsed with excitement. But Savrola, as surely Holmes himself would have done, 'had put on the armour of his philosophy and gazed on the world as from a distance'.

Churchill was never to publish another novel and never again to show so clearly his literary origins in the thought and feeling of the nineties. But it is the case that in one respect he continued, as a writer, to emulate his surrogate Savrola. For in all that he subsequently wrote, and in a way that involved a certain kind of English prose style, a certain fatalism and a certain stoicism, he would always, as we will see, 'put on the armour of his philosophy'.

II

Churchill was not in England when the first reviews of *Savrola* appeared. In the autumn of 1899 war had broken out between the British and the Boers in South Africa. The event provided just the kind of opportunity that Churchill, the now professional writer, wanted. He set out for South Africa immediately.

As a result of the success of *The River War* he obtained from the *Morning Post* a lucrative contract to report the fighting. Longmans would continue to publish his work in book form. At the age of twenty-five he was a recognised and professional writer.

But even more rewarding for Churchill's larger career were the things that happened to him during his time in South Africa. He was taken prisoner by the Boers and held in a prison camp in Pretoria, from which he escaped. This happened at a time when Britain was suffering severe reverses in the war. The result was that Churchill's escape made him the pretext for a long-needed patriotic celebration; he became a national hero and a national and international celebrity overnight.

Churchill's next two books are made up of the letters dispatched to the *Morning Post* from South Africa. They describe Churchill's own highly dramatic experiences and also the larger campaigns in which these figured. The first, *London to Ladysmith via Pretoria*, describes in great detail the long and difficult struggle of the British and imperial forces to lift the siege of Ladysmith in the first few months of 1900. And the second book, and very much a sequel, *Ian Hamilton's March*, is another sequence of letters which reports the progress of one of the armies under Lord Roberts as it pushes the Boers northward and finally captures Pretoria and Johannesburg in the spring of that same year.

In these two books Churchill is very conscious of himself as the established journalist and war correspondent. Speaking of his special role in the war in South Africa he writes, jocularly, of the dangers which 'attend a War Correspondent's precarious existence. This I recognise as a necessary evil, for the lot of the writer in the field is a hard and heavy one. "All the danger of war and one-half per cent, the glory": such is our motto, and this is the reason why we expect large salaries.' He is also very aware of the technical difficulties of his trade at this moment in the history of journalism. 'Alas! the days of newspaper enterprise in war are over. What can one do with a censor, a forty-eight hours' delay and a fifty-word limit on the wire?' And, as in *The River War*, he is quick to pay tribute to those whom he regards as the great and skilled practitioners of journalism. Three pages, for instance, are devoted to the abilities of G.W. Steevens whom, years later, in his autobiography Churchill would recall as 'the most brilliant man in journalism I have ever met'. When Steevens dies of the fever that infected the garrison of Ladysmith, Churchill grieves for his loss as a man and as a journalist. 'His conversation and his private letters sparkled like his books and articles. Original expressions, just similitudes, striking phrases, quaint or droll ideas welled in his mind without the slightest effort . . . His wit was the genuine article –

absolutely natural and spontaneous.' Churchill also recalls his colleague's bravery and self-effacement as a journalist. He was in the forefront of one of the intensest battles in the Egyptian campaign and 'He wrote a vivid account of the attack, but there was nothing in it about himself.'

There is no such impersonality or modesty in Churchill's coverage of the South African War. In these two books there is, in fact, as in so many of his other works, a strong autobiographical thread. Certainly he reports the battles in great detail and he gives the reader an excellent sense of the South African townships and the landscape that the British army passes through. But continually he returns to his own thoughts and feelings and experiences. He reports in considerable detail his capture by the Boers and his escape from the prison camp. Perhaps it could be said that these were newsworthy stories meriting the attention of a journalist. But this would not be true of, say, the spiritual experience, the recourse to prayer that occurred when he was on the run from the Boers, when he 'realised with awful force that no exercise of my own feeble wit and strength could save me from my enemies and that without the assistance of that High Power which interferes in the eternal sequence of causes and effects more often than we are always prone to admit, I could never succeed'. And now, abandoning the Gibbonian scepticism of his earlier books, he adds in a simple, forceful sentence, 'I prayed long and earnestly for help and guidance.' He also writes vividly of his experience of 'the hateful degradation of imprisonment'. The anger that he felt at the humiliations inflicted by one of his captors in particular, a Mr Malan, pulses strongly in his writing.

At one point in the second volume of letters Churchill feels it necessary to pause to acquit himself of the possible charge of seeking out all the dangers, escapes and adventures that befell him during these campaigns. This ambitious young man is sensitive to the accusation of self-advertisement. And he proceeds to describe what was his most perilous experience in South Africa – one that was by no means sought out – the occasion when he was thrown by his bolting horse as the Boer marksmen drew close and he was saved by a British cavalryman who stopped to let him mount up behind him, for which action his saviour was nominated for the VC. The personal experience which is at the centre of the second book about South Africa, *Ian Hamilton's March*, is an internal rather than external one. For in one important respect this book is a book about a youthful admiration. The general whose name appears in the title and to whom it is dedicated is for Churchill the perfect modern instance of the hero.

In the course of the narration we see General Hamilton in many military situations and we hear him in conversations. And one of the letters in the very middle of the book, and one written when Churchill had returned to England and was revising his reports, is an essay of nearly thirty pages on the life and the qualities of this revered leader. Churchill traces Hamilton's career from his days at Sandhurst to his years of service in India and his courageous and daring achievements in the first Boer War, in which an enemy rifle-shot destroyed his hand and wrist, resulting in what Churchill terms 'a glorious deformity'. On his return to India, Hamilton became an aide-de-camp to the overall commander General Roberts and was swiftly promoted. He also served in the Sudan before returning to South Africa to serve in the second war against the Boers. Churchill greatly commends his hero's 'personal gallantry and military conduct' in this war and lists numerous occasions of achievement in which Hamilton was involved. The climax comes with what Churchill calls 'the Homeric contest', 'when the British General and Commandant Prinslow of the Free State fired at each other at five yards' range.'

Churchill was a ready critic of generals. The young journalist was, as we have seen, quite ready to express his reservations about aspects of Kitchener's conduct in the Sudan. He also questions some of the policies of Sir Redvers Buller in the war in South Africa. But in the case of Ian Hamilton Churchill has no reservations whatsoever, only intense and sympathetic understanding. It is as though the 25-year-old Churchill makes a very special identification with this senior officer who is twenty-one years older than he. Hamilton, like Churchill, had to wangle his way into the Sudan war. Like Churchill, he had to use determination and cunning to defeat a military bureaucracy which had turned him down. He is a good instance of Churchill's dictum 'You do not rise by the regulations, but in spite of them.' One occasion of such identification occurs as Hamilton's army approaches the Boer defences south of Johannesburg. Churchill confesses to anxiety, 'to a beating heart', but notices that the General is completely calm. 'But the man who bore all the responsibility, and to whom the result meant everything, appeared utterly unmoved.' Recalling his effort at self-reassurance, Churchill writes, 'I could almost imagine myself the General and the General the Press Correspondent, though perhaps this arrangement would scarcely have worked so well.'

Another reason for Churchill's special feeling for Ian Hamilton was that both were men of literary gifts and interests. At one point in his career Hamilton had, in fact, wondered whether 'he should leave the army and throw himself entirely into the literary pursuits which had always possessed for him a keen attraction'. In the event, he remained a soldier but he did manage to write as well. He published a volume of verses deriving from his time in India entitled *The Ballad of Hadji and the Boar* and a prose work describing a sailing voyage down the west coast of India entitled *A Jaunt in a Junk*. Churchill reports that Hamilton also cultivated acquaintance with men of letters. We are again reminded of his and Hamilton's literary roots in the nineties when he tells us that one of these acquaintances was Andrew Lang, best remembered today as the author of the series of children's books beginning with the *Blue Fairy Tale Book* of 1889. Churchill also reprints a twelve-line poem 'To Colonel Hamilton' which Andrew Lang used to dedicate a volume of poems to him. Lang's 'compulsive lines' express the same near adulation for Hamilton that Churchill himself felt for his fellow soldier-writer who had among his many other gifts, according to Churchill, 'a fine taste in words'.

For the frontispiece to the book Churchill chose to reproduce a portrait of Hamilton by Sargent. In his eighth chapter he pauses to meditate on the portrait. It shows 'a man of rather more than middle height, spare, keen-eyed, and of commanding aspect. His highly nervous temperament animating what appears a frail body imparts to all his movement a kind of feverish energy.' As description changes into tribute Churchill asserts, 'To his personal charm as a companion, to his temper never ruffled or vexed either by internal irritation or the stir and contrariness of events, his friends and those who have served under him will bear witness.'

Ian Hamilton's March is an account of a military campaign. It is at the same time a memoir of someone who constituted a major experience, a major influence, in the life of the 25-year-old Winston Churchill.

Such deep personal involvement in the narrative is what endows *Ian Hamilton's March* with more than journalistic or historical interest. It gives it a definite literary interest and value. In this respect it is similar to a book about war written by someone with a radically different background, political outlook and prose style from Churchill's. I refer to George Orwell, who in his account of the campaign of the Catalan anarchists against Franco in the Spanish Civil War gives us, as well as military reportage, a chapter of his own autobiography. *Homage To Catalonia* has in fact many features in common with *Ian Hamilton's March*. It would be in no way misleading if Churchill's book were to be titled 'Homage to Ian Hamilton'. Both authors set out as war correspondents, Churchill with an actual commission from a newspaper, Orwell hoping (misguidedly, as it turned out) to sell his reports to the *New Statesman*. Both authors become involved with the experience of an army and both are affected by the admiration which they develop for certain individuals in the course of a difficult campaign. Both books end with a salute and a sense of loss as the authors leave their companions with whom they have marched and fought. Both books have a chief thematic preoccupation with the nature of heroism, though, of course, heroism took different forms in two such different twentieth-century wars as the second Boer War and the Spanish Civil War.

Churchill and Orwell both have assured places in the history of English prose in this century. But as one way of formulating Churchill's literary achievement one can say that at its best his writing is much more alive and responsive than anything in Orwell's three volumes of reportage, *Down And Out In Paris And London*, *The Road To Wigan Pier* and *Homage To Catalonia*. I do not think there is anywhere in these Orwell books a passage to match the following as a piece of descriptive prose. (Churchill is describing how, after his escape from the Boer prison camp, he jumped on to a train that he hoped would carry him to Portuguese East Africa and to freedom.)

> The train started slowly, but gathered speed sooner than I had expected. The flaring lights drew swiftly near. The rattle grew into a roar. The dark mass hung for a second above me. The engine-driver silhouetted against his furnace glow, the black profile of the engine, the clouds of steam rushed past. Then I hurled myself on the trucks, clutching at something, missed, clutched again, missed again, grasped some sort of hand-hold, was swung off my feet – my toes bumping on the line, and with a struggle seated myself on the couplings of the fifth truck from the front of the train. It was a goods train, and the trucks were full of sacks, soft sacks covered with coal dust. I crawled on top and burrowed in among them. In five minutes I was completely buried. The sacks were warm and comfortable. Perhaps the engine-driver had seen me rush up to the train and would give the alarm at the next station: on the other hand, perhaps not. Where was the train going to? Where would it be unloaded? Would it be searched?

The rush of panicky questions at the last, like the action details at the beginning made up of a quick succession of short, simple sentences, is language as accurate and close as it is possible to be to the actuality of intense and dramatic experience. The sixth sentence, the compound sentence, employs all the art of syntactical pace to convey the second-by-second uncertainty and apprehension during the moments just before, and then during, the leap on to the train.

Churchill's subsequent development as a writer would take him away from this sort of description of physical adventure; his long career as a prose writer was to be a many-sided one. But his two books about South Africa show not just promise in this kind of writing, they constitute a genuine literary achievement. *Ian Hamilton's March* (1900) marks the end of what is very distinctly the first phase of Churchill's literary career. It stands at the end of a startlingly energetic literary debut in which the ambitious young writer had published five books in just two years.

But in 1900 writing took second place to politics when Churchill the writer and war celebrity was elected to the House of Commons as Tory member for Oldham. Not for another six years would he publish his next book. And this, his biography of his father, that other hero of his early life, would deal with a new and different kind of experience, would be brought out by a different publisher and would entail the undertaking of a different kind of prose.

CHAPTER THREE

Biographer and Travel Writer

I

Churchill made his maiden speech very early on in the session that began in February 1901. Thereafter he spoke regularly in the House, making himself heard and felt on several issues; he also on occasion put himself to the fore in the correspondence column of *The Times*. In Parliament he was very much aware of following in his father's footsteps. One of his initial parliamentary concerns was with an issue that had contributed to the fall of Lord Randolph, retrenchment in military expenditure. In one of his early speeches to the House he quoted from memory passages from his father's letter of resignation to Lord Salisbury, and concluded his own protest against the current defence budget by declaring, 'I think it is about time that a voice . . . should . . . protest against the policy of daily increasing the public burden . . . I say it humbly, but with I hope becoming pride, no one has a better right than I have, for this is a cause I have inherited, and a cause for which the late Lord Randolph Churchill made the greatest sacrifice of any Minister of modern times.'

Churchill also followed his father in becoming a member of what had the appearance of being a splinter group within the Tory parliamentary party. This was a group of young aristocrats led by the Marquess of Salisbury's son, Hugh Cecil, and known as the Hughligans or Hooligans. Cecil, like another member of the set, Lord Percy, was very much a Tory intellectual. Churchill remembered him as a figure from Disraeli's novels. He was 'a thoughtful and romantic youth . . . of great personal charm and academic achievement'. (He had won the Newdigate Prize at Oxford.) Though still a very young man, 'He had travelled widely in the highlands of Asia Minor and the Caucasus feasting with princely barbarians and fasting with priestly fanatics. Over him the East exercised the spell it cast over Disraeli. He might, indeed, have stepped out of the pages of Tancred or Coningsby.'

For Churchill and these sophisticated and travelled young men the Tory front bench came to seem lacklustre. They got into the habit of associating and socialising with members of the right wing of the Liberal opposition such as Asquith, Haldane, Sir Edward Grey and Lord Randolph's old friend, the historian, biographer and highly successful racehorse owner, Lord Rosebery. Churchill himself grew still more disenchanted with the Conservatives when the party came under the influence of Joesph Chamberlain's passion for Imperial Preference, a common market of the British Empire. This became one of the chief issues in British politics in the first decade of this century. It was an idea that would be promoted in various guises until the time of Britain's entry into the European Economic Community in the seventies. A life-long proponent of economic protection for the Empire was the Canadian imperialist, the writer and newspaper magnate Max Aitken, later Lord Beaverbrook, soon to become Churchill's personal friend and, years later, an important political ally.

But in the early years of this century Churchill detested Chamberlain's policy of imperial preference. In one of the first of his many memorable speeches to the House of Commons, he delivered in the spring of 1905 a lengthy and detailed attack on the government's policy of protectionism, concluding with the words:

> . . . it rests on no moral, logical, or scientific foundation. It does not make for prosperity, it does not make for international peace . . . we do not want to see the British Empire degenerate into a sullen confederacy, walled off, like a medieval town, from the surrounding country; victualled for a siege, and containing within the circle of its battlements all that is necessary for war. We want this country and the States associated with it to take their parts freely and fairly in the general intercourse of commercial nations. We do not mind even if we have become dependent on foreign nations, because we know that by that very fact we make foreign nations dependent upon us.

Such views made it increasingly difficult for Churchill to continue as a Tory MP. There was much uneasiness in his constituency at Oldham. And there were growing tensions, political, social and personal, with his fellow-Conservatives at Westminster. The developing animosities came to a head in the House of Commons at the end of March 1904. The occasion constituted one of the most acutely painful experiences in Churchill's career so far. It precipitated the tormenting decision to abandon the political party in which he had grown up and to go over to the Liberals, whom both as politician and as writer (in *The Malakand Field Force* and *The River War*) he had criticised and condemned.

What happened that day was this: when the speaker called upon Churchill to address the House, the whole of the Tory party, led by the Prime Minister, Arthur Balfour, stood up and walked out of the House. Churchill was, on his own admission, greatly shocked by this well-organised demonstration; so much so that he found it difficult to proceed with his speech. The following day he wrote to a friend:

> . . . in the House yesterday . . . I was the object of a very unpleasant and disconcerting demonstration. I would far rather have been rudely interrupted for I might have placated that kind of opposition, or at the worst, laughed at it. But the feeling of the whole audience melting behind one and being left with crowded Liberal benches and an absolutely empty Government side was most disquieting, and it was only by a considerable effort that I forced myself to proceed to the end of my remarks.

A further indication of Tory anger at Churchill's Free Trade views came some days later when, whilst speaking in the House, his concentration completely left him and he had stumblingly to apologise to the House and abruptly sit down. As he did so he heard the laughter and mockery of some of the younger Tory members. (Older and kinder members recalled sadly that Lord Randolph Churchill had often collapsed in similar fashion in his last speeches in the House.) In just one month Churchill made the clearly traumatic decision to cross the floor and sit on the Liberal benches. He chose the seat, just below the gangway, where his father had sat when in opposition. Winston Churchill had then been a Conservative MP for little more than four years.

It seems unlikely that this action was entirely a matter of opinions concerning the financial specifics or the larger morality of Free Trade as opposed to Imperial Preference. The decision had also an emotional, a psychological, indeed a literary side to it. In Churchill's first few years in Parliament he slowly developed a personal antipathy to many of his fellow-Conservatives and especially to the Prime

Minister, the languid, dilettante and somewhat ethereal amateur philosopher Arthur Balfour. Above all he always had in his mind what he regarded as the party's betrayal of his father. The figures with seniority in the Conservative party in the early 1900s, the men who were Winston's political chiefs, were the very ones who had abandoned Lord Randolph nearly twenty years before. The resentment grated. After finally joining the Liberals the thirty-year-old Winston wrote, 'When I think of all the labours Lord Randolph Churchill gave to the fortunes of the Conservative Party and the ungrateful way in which he was treated by them when they obtained the power they would never have had but for him, I am delighted that circumstances have enabled me to break with them while I am still young and still have the first energies of my life to give to the popular cause.'

One very clear reason why he was so aware of his father and his father's parliamentary fortunes at this period of his own highly dramatic political evolution was that he was, during these very years 1902–1905, engaged in the researching and the writing of his father's biography. And, of course, to write a biography is in some ways like reliving the life of the subject. He began work on the book in the summer of 1902, when his dissatisfactions with the Conservative party were developing, and he completed the writing in 1905, the year after he had gone over to the Liberals. A political process went along with a literary process. And it is clear that some of the insights achieved in the latter affected the former. The findings and feelings of the writer informed those of the politician.

To undertake the book Churchill had to obtain the approval of his father's literary executors headed by Lord Rosebery. Churchill promised that he would devote himself to this act of filial piety with 'reverence and industry'. And so he did. He made a thorough study of numerous large tin boxes containing his father's papers. He approached many of his father's contemporaries, asking them to supply him with further evidence. The young biographer even solicited recollections from the nearly seventy-year-old Joseph Chamberlain, the imperialist protectionist, who was at this time very much his political opponent. Churchill, in fact, in the midst of the great political and emotional turmoil in his own life, had a pleasant visit to Highbury, the great mansion Chamberlain had had built for himself in suburban Birmingham. The two dined together and split a bottle of vintage port and went over old letters and memories. Churchill was touched by his magnanimous reception by this phenomenally energetic maverick of late Victorian political life. 'He got out the Cup which my father gave him on his third marriage and made a great fuss about it and generally I preserve very pleasant recollections of a most interesting episode . . .'

On completing his more than three years' work as a biographer, Churchill chose as his literary agent Frank Harris, the editor and writer who was later to become famous, if not infamous, for his memoirs, *My Life And Loves*. Harris obtained for Churchill a contract that at that time was extremely lucrative. The book was sold to Macmillan for an advance of £8,000, a figure which Churchill's first publishers felt unable to match. The two-volume work was published in early January 1906, the same year as John Galsworthy's *Man of Property* and Conrad's *The Secret Agent* appeared.

The biography of Lord Randolph runs to more than a thousand pages, excluding the several appendices in which Winston published certain of his father's political papers. It is a very large work, one to be ranked with those other very substantial volumes that characterise biography as a literary form in its Victorian and Edwardian phases. In length and stateliness of style it has much in common with Rosebery's *Life of Pitt* and Morley's *Life of Gladstone*. It is very much a political biography. Certainly the author makes a few remarks on his subject's boyhood and youth, touching on his two continental tours, his boisterousness at Merton College Oxford and his smashing of the windows of the Randolph Hotel in that city. He also describes his youthful passion for the hunt and his involvement with the Blenheim Harriers, which stood him in good stead with the farmers around Woodstock when later in life he came to solicit their votes. But important personal experiences such as Lord Randolph's marriage and the social ostracising of the couple demanded by the Prince of Wales (whom Winston does not name) are touched on only briefly.

The exiling to Ireland – which followed on the Prince's ban – where Randolph served as secretary to his father, the Duke of Marlborough, who was appointed Lord Lieutenant, receives rather more attention, since Randolph's many travels throughout Ireland and his numerous conversations with people at all levels of Irish society prepared him to be a very informed participant in all the great debates on Home Rule during his subsequent years in Parliament. Out of such experience came his decision 'to play the orange card' in 1886, when he encouraged and promised support to Ulster Protestants in their refusal to participate in an Ireland placed under Home Rule.

After the first fifty pages the biography is almost entirely political in its concerns. The remainder of the thousand and more pages relates in great detail, sometimes day by day, Lord Randolph's political fortunes from the time he entered the House of Commons in 1874, the same year in which his son Winston was born. But the writing is such as still today to compel the interest of readers not especially versed in the political and parliamentary minutiae of the 1880s and early 1890s. For it tells a very dramatic story, the story of a glamorous and spectacular political success swiftly followed by nemesis and humiliation. That it is a very long book does not detract from its overall readability. Some good reads are very long reads. Ruskin's *Stones Of Venice*, for instance, is far more impressive, far more of a reading experience when read as a totality rather than in excerpts. Churchill's thousand pages almost always have a strong narrative drive and the members of the supporting cast of characters are vividly particularised.

Winston Churchill was eleven years old when his father performed the brilliant feat, unusual in those or any days, of becoming both Chancellor of the Exchequer and Leader of the House of Commons at the age of thirty-seven (The achievement of this youthful political prodigy is comparable to that of John F. Kennedy some three-quarters of a century later.) The years that led up to this great personal success for Lord Randolph were the years of Winston's childhood. The future biographer would have only an imperfect understanding of what was going on. But his father's subsequent fall and humiliation were a part of Winston's teenage experience and, as the writing in this book shows, affected him deeply.

Lord Randolph's years of political ascent are ones into which, with the aid of written evidence, Winston tries to imagine himself. He frequently dwells on occasions that show Lord Randolph's powers of attracting great crowds and dominating them with his oratory. Here, for instance, is Winston's account of how his father at the height of his political celebrity 'played the orange card' in Northern Ireland in 1886:

> Lord Randolph crossed the Channel and arrived at Larne early on the morning of 22 February. He was welcomed like a king. Thousands of persons, assembling from the neighbouring townships, greeted him at the port . . . In Belfast itself a vast demonstration, remarkable for its earnestness and quality and amounting, it is computed, to more than seventy thousand people, marched past him. One who knew Ireland well declared that he had not believed 'there were so many Orangemen in the world'. That night the Ulster Hall was crowded to its utmost compass. In order to satisfy the demand for tickets all the seats were removed and the concourse which he addressed for nearly an hour and a half – heard him standing. He was nearly always successful on the platform, but the effect he produced upon his audience in Belfast was one of the most

> memorable triumphs of his life. He held the meeting in the hollow of his hand. From the very centre of Protestant excitement he appealed to the loyal Catholics of Ireland to stand firm by the Union and at the same time, without using any language of bigotry or intolerance, he roused the Orangemen to stern and vehement emotion.

Winston Churchill also dwells on the charismatic appeal which his father, the Tory Democrat, had for members of the working class, especially the young ones.

> In times when good Conservatives despaired of the fortunes of their party under a democratic franchise and even making a virtue of necessity, regarded it as almost immoral to court a working class vote and . . . when Liberal orators and statesmen . . . were looking forward to an election which should relegate the Conservative party to the limbo of obsolete ideas, they were disconcerted by the spectacle, repeatedly presented, of multitudes of working men hanging upon the words of a young aristocrat . . . Wherever he went he was received by tremendous throngs and with extraordinary demonstrations of goodwill.

This was the same young aristocrat who just a few years before, when he was twenty-three, had been, as Winston pictures him,

> markedly reserved in his manner to acquaintances, utterly unguarded to his intimate friends, something of a dandy in his dress, an earnest sportsman, an omnivorous reader, moving with a jaunty step through what were in those days the very select circles of fashion and clubland, seeking the pleasure of the Turf and town.

Winston Churchill attributes his father's abandonment of this sort of life and his founding of Tory Democracy to his exclusion from London high society at the insistence of the Prince of Wales.

> The fashionable world no longer smiled. Powerful enemies were anxious to humiliate him. His own sensitiveness and pride magnified every coldness into an affront. London became odious to him . . . a nature originally genial and gay contracted a stern and bitter quality, a harsh contempt for what is called 'Society', and an abiding antagonism to rank and authority. If this misfortune produced in Lord Randolph characteristics which afterwards hindered or injured his public work, it was also his spur. Without it he might have wasted a dozen years in the frivolous and expensive pursuits of the silly world of fashion; without it he would probably never have developed popular sympathies or the courage to champion democratic causes.

As he traces his father's career as leader of the Fourth Party and of Tory Democracy, Winston ponders the oratorical and literary skills which attracted so many enthusiastic supporters to Lord Randolph. He speaks of 'the forcible homely English of which he was a natural master', of 'the veins of rough spontaneous mirth which characterise the style and language of his rhetoric and writings'. He would, writes Winston, 'toss and gore fools with true Johnsonian vigour and zest'. 'Wit, abuse, epigrams, imagery, argument – all were "Randolphian". No one else said the same kind of things, or said them in the same kind of way. He possessed the strange quality, unconsciously exerted and not by any means to be simulated, of compelling attention . . .' 'As Tacitus said of Mucianus, "*Omnium quae dixerat, feveratque, arte quadam ostentator*" ("He had the showman's knack of drawing public attention to everything he said or did").'

The reference to Tacitus here is not the only one in the biography, which embraces a range of literary allusions far greater than in any of Churchill's previous books. It is one of the aspects of the style of the work that makes the biographer, still only in his very early thirties, appear to the reader as judicious, humane and indeed wise. As well as to classical writers such as Tacitus and Horace we are referred to Goethe, Machiavelli, Emerson, Pope, Carlyle, Montaigne and Byron. Altogether they constitute a range of literary and humane wisdom rare in a political biography.

There are two pivotal chapters in the high drama (some of Churchill's imagery implies the high tragedy)[1] of Lord Randolph's career. Each has its theme underlined by an important epigraph. The first of these chapters, entitled 'Resignation', has as its epigraph eight lines from Dryden. Winston Churchill notes that these lines were copied out by Lord Randolph 'about 1891', some five years after his resignation and the ruin of his career. Churchill remarks towards the end of the biography that 'there is an air of musty tragedy about old letters'. We sense his acute sadness as he turns over his father's papers. A similar feeling is elicited by discovering his father's transcription from Dryden. The lines read:

> Happy the man, and happy he alone,
> He who can call to-day his own –
> He who, secure within, can say:
> To-morrow do thy worst, for I have lived to-day.
> Come fair or foul, or rain or shine,

[1] There is, for instance, a clear reference to the fall of King Lear when Churchill depicts metaphorically his father's resignation as a matter of going 'forth into the night storm almost alone . . .'

> The joys I have possessed, in spite of fate, are mine.
> Not Heaven itself over the past hath power;
> But what has been has been, and I have had my hour.

In the chapter that follows these lines of calm, even proud, acceptance of a life of anti-climax, Winston Churchill relates and seeks to explain to himself and to the reader his father's ruin as a result of his sudden and precipitate relinquishing of two of the highest offices of state. It contains a very interesting anatomy of the Tory party of that time and draws upon Lord Randolph's own distinction between governing, which he believed the Tory party of that day could do, and legislating, which it could not. Winston also makes a vividly succinct contrast between the personalities of his father, the would-be legislator, and Lord Salisbury, the Prime Minister, to whom he submitted his resignation and who represented the other kind of late Victorian Conservatism.

> Neither could be insensible to the personal fascination of the other. Both rejoiced in a wide and illuminating survey of public affairs; both dwelt much upon the future; both preserved a cynical disdain of small men seeking paltry ends. But the gulf which separated the fiery leader of Tory Democracy – with his bold plans of reform and dreams of change, with his record of storm and triumph and slender expectations of a long life – from the old-fashioned Conservative statesman, the head of a High Church and High Tory family, versed in diplomacy, representative of authority, wary, austere, content to govern – was a gulf no mutual needs, no common interests, no personal likings could permanently bridge. They represented conflicting schools of political philosophy. They stood for ideas mutually incompatible. Sooner or later the breach must have come; and no doubt the strong realisation of this underlay the action of the one and the acquiescence of the other.

As he ponders the ending of his father's 'hour' and his resignation submitted on the grounds of the unacceptability of the Navy and Army estimates, Winston never criticises his father. In one sentence he speaks of him acting 'quixotically' and in another he says, 'But still a more patient man would have waited.' He also considers the view that after the resignation Lord Randolph should have made a clean break and completely given up a political life. That way he would not have been the victim, that he became, of his former colleagues' bitterness, scorn and abuse.

> He should have stated the whole grounds of his difference with the Tory Cabinet, minimising nothing, keeping nothing back. In two or

> three speeches in Parliament and the country he should broadly have outlined his general political conception of the course the Conservative party should follow, and then, unless he was prepared to wage relentless war upon the Government for the purpose of compelling them to adopt that course, he should forthwith have withdrawn himself from public life.

But this hypothesis concerning Lord Randolph's self-preservation is as close as we come to any reservations on the biographer's part. For the rest Winston portrays his father, as he had done Savrola, as a noble, generous, visionary idealist who is compromised by lesser people. 'Austere Conservatives [who] shrank from this alarming representative of the New Democracy. Worthy men thoughtlessly slighted, tiresome people ruthlessly snubbed, office-seekers whose pretensions had been ignored, Parliamentary martinets concerned for party discipline, all were held in check only so long as he was powerful.' But once he had failed to implement his left-wing policies and had resigned, he became forever the butt and victim of such people. In some powerful rhetorical questions heavy with bathos the biographer conveys the shocking rapidity of his father's change of fortune:

> Who could have guessed that ruin, utter and irretrievable, was marching swiftly upon this triumphant figure; that the great party that had followed his lead so blithely would in a few brief months turn upon him in abiding displeasure; and that the Parliament which had assembled to find him so powerful and to accept his guidance, would watch him creep away in sadness and alone?

If the biographer's style works to dramatise the situation in this way, it can also convey an almost painful empathising with Lord Randolph's condition as when, for instance, Winston remembers, lingering on distressing adjectives, how '. . . he delivered himself, unarmed, unattended, fettered even, to his enemies; and therefrom ensued not only his political ruin; but grave injury to the causes he sustained'.

These words, like so many others in the biography, convey some of the author's compassion for his father's sudden vulnerability. It is a feeling which together with disgust at the subsequent behaviour of Lord Randolph's enemies dominates the concluding chapters of the book. The very next chapter, 'The Turn Of The Tide', begins the story of Lord Randolph's political isolation and decline. The epigraph is from Francis Bacon, a writer to whom Winston Churchill also refers often in his letters. The Jacobean trenchancy of the sentence is an excellent encapsulation of Lord Randolph's story. It reads: 'The rising unto place is laborious . . . the standing is slippery, and the regress is either a downfall or at least an eclipse which is a melancholy thing.'

During the rest of Lord Randolph's life, writes Winston, 'he encountered nothing but disappointment and failure'. It is true that he retained the support and affection of working-class Tories, especially in the North. Winston reports at some length and with evident pleasure an occasion on which his father attracted a vast crowd to a speech he gave at an outdoor meeting at Whitby. Prominent local Tories behaved insultingly to Lord Randolph and refused to attend his meeting. However, 'The 7,000 persons who gathered upon the sands and around the slopes of a kind of natural amphitheatre under the west cliff gave him a very different welcome, and listened with delighted attention during that beautiful afternoon.' But otherwise his political standing continued to deteriorate. Criticism of Conservative policy which he made in later years would quickly revive the mockery, contempt and charges of treachery directed towards him. Like another very charismatic speaker, Aneurin Bevan, who brought on himself hostility that led to excrement being sent to him in the mail, Lord Randolph could bring upon himself an inordinate and infuriated hatred from his former supporters. He was especially vilified and baited for his vehement objections to the government's setting up of a judicial commission to investigate charges of violence and conspiracy brought against Parnell and other Irishmen.

Winston Churchill describes how his father was baited at this time. He was 'discussed with general malice by the Conservative newspapers. He was burlesqued on the Gaiety stage with a wit so pointed that the song was stopped by the intervention of the Lord Chamberlain . . . paragraphs, lampoons and caricatures exhibited him daily to the ridicule of his countrymen . . . delegates of the National Union hooted his name at their annual conference . . . and . . . the chiefs of the Tories complacently admired the fullness of their triumph.' The bitter mockery reported here by Churchill he would himself have witnessed. For it occurred in 1891, the year in which Winston was seventeen. The experience must have helped to account for that feeling for nemesis which marks the last chapters of the book. For, only a very few years before, Winston had sent letters from Harrow begging his father, then the coming politician and popular celebrity, to send autographs for him to give to his schoolmates.

There is a strong element of poetry in the prose of this biography. Certainly there is a very detailed account of every political action or occasion of any significance in Lord Randolph's life, even down to a lengthy consideration of the budget speech which his resignation as

Chancellor of the Exchequer prevented him from giving. But the book is more than just a narrative of political doings. The prose in which the story is told is expressive of many feelings: compassion, anger, sadness. At the last, as the terrible illness ends Lord Randolph's dignity and then his life, there comes a mood and tone of elegy. But the concluding paragraphs, and certainly the very last one, switch suddenly to a tone of pride and defiance as Winston Churchill salutes his father and the particular idea of England to which his father adhered. This is not the England of those whom Winston in a contemptuous archaism disparages as 'fuglemen' or drill sergeants. Rather it is an England of the independent, liberal, thoughtful centre. It is similar to the vision of England that concludes E.M. Forster's novel *Howards End*, published a couple of years after this biography. It is an idea of England which was to attract Winston Churchill, sometime Tory, sometime Liberal, as it had attracted his father. The long biography ends with the assertion of this idea:

> There is an England which stretches far beyond the well-drilled masses who are assembled by party machinery to salute with appropriate acclamation the utterances of their recognised fuglemen; an England of wise men who gaze without self-deception at the failings and follies of both political parties; of brave and earnest men who find in neither faction fair scope for the effort that is in them; of 'poor men' who increasingly doubt the sincerity of party philanthropy. It was to that England that Lord Randolph Churchill appealed; it was that England he so nearly won; it is by that England he will be justly judged.

II

The month after the biography of his father was published, Winston Churchill the Liberal returned to Parliament as a junior minister in the newly elected Liberal government. He was Under-Secretary for the Colonies, serving under Lord Elgin. It is a mark of the speed of Churchill's political advancement that just seven years before, when Churchill was a very junior officer in India, Lord Elgin was Viceroy. The Colonial Secretary was the grandson of the Earl of Elgin, who had acquired the Elgin marbles, and the son of a Governor-General of Canada. But for all his political and administrative pedigree Elgin was not a very energetic Colonial Secretary. He spent a good deal of his time on his estate in Scotland tending his wife, who had born him eleven children and was, understandably, in frail health.

Elgin's many absences from Parliament meant that Churchill enjoyed greater prominence in the management of colonial affairs than might otherwise have been the case. He was very active as a frontbencher in the House of Commons, where he often clashed violently with former associates in the Conservative opposition, particularly on matters to do with postwar reconciliation in and with South Africa. (His extensive knowledge of that country, as demonstrated in his books and speeches, was one reason for his governmental appointment.) Churchill also worked his permanent under-secretary Sir Francis Hopwood very hard and incurred his resentment. Sir Francis wrote of him, 'He is most tiresome to deal with and will, I fear, give trouble – as his father did – in any position to which he may be called. The restless energy, uncontrollable desire for notoriety and lack of moral perception make him an anxiety indeed.'

Churchill was prominent in an important colonial conference in 1907, in which year he was also made a privy councillor, and set off in an official capacity, and followed by the press, to visit British colonial possessions in East Africa. On this journey he was accompanied by a

The advertisement for Churchill's fifth book, published in 1908 when he was thirty-three.

few friends including his recently appointed secretary Edward Marsh, who, like that other life-long friend, Ian Hamilton, was a man of strong literary interests. From this expedition there derived Churchill's next book, the collection of travel pieces, *My African Journey*. The work began as a series of articles, which were sold to the *Strand Magazine* by Churchill's literary agent A.P. Watt, and subsequently put together as a book and published by Hodder & Stoughton in the following year, 1908.

The eleven essays constitute a very pleasing travel book but not one of Churchill's major works of prose. They show him for the first time in what will from now on be one of his permanent roles, the famous man. The soldier, the journalist, the writer, the volatile politician has now also become the public personage. He is received by British and African dignitaries, he makes speeches and, his mother writes to tell him, his tour is reported amusingly in *Punch*. In the articles in the book he discusses some of the current political issues facing East Africa. He also supplies some fine, atmospheric descriptions of differing landscapes in that part of the continent. He makes jokes. As a man of letters he refers to Dante and Ruskin and Carlyle and H.G. Wells. As a junior minister he makes party political points, reminding us, for instance, that the Uganda Railway 'one of the most romantic and most wonderful railways in the world' is 'the adventurous enterprise of a Liberal Government'. And in one passage of political comment he recommends 'a practical experiment in State Socialism'.

He also devotes several of the essays to an account of his adventures and successes as a big-game hunter. To ecology-conscious readers at the end of the twentieth century these reports of the shooting for sport of rare wild animals must seem shocking. The hunting descriptions more than anything else in the book show up the gap between the conventions of the prosperous Edwardian male traveler, or even those of Ernest Hemingway's time, and those of most Western people today. But ecology aside, the essays read entertainingly. 'Essays' though, is not really the proper term for them. For they are not carefully designed and structured as Churchill's essays will be when, later in life, as consciously an essayist, he turns to this particular prose form. The pieces in *My African Journey*, his shortest book to date (about 130 pages), are more a sequence of jottings, more *ad hoc*. They move along from landscape descriptions to philosophising to curiosities and trivia to political reflections. Reading the sequence of articles is like being with Churchill on his African tour, seeing what he saw and sharing his often quite discontinuous thoughts and feelings.

Upon his return to London in March 1908 Churchill commissioned Rowland Ward Ltd, taxidermists of Piccadilly, to treat his hunting trophies. There were seven heads, including one of a rhinoceros, and also three zebra skins. But within weeks his attention was diverted from his safari haul by more serious matters. The Prime Minister, Campbell Bannerman, became too ill to continue in office and was succeeded by Henry Asquith. In the government reshuffle Churchill was made President of the Board of Trade. It was an office which brought with it promotion to cabinet rank. He was thirty-three years old. In his political career, as in his writing career, he was a youthful prodigy.

CHAPTER FOUR

Among Literary Liberals

I

At the very same time that he became a member of the Liberal government, in December 1905, Churchill also began one of those several friendships which were to form such an important part of his life. This one, which was to last for nearly half a century, was the most enduring of them. It was also to bring to Churchill a relationship with, and access to, the literary world of the England of the time.

Just before Christmas of that year Churchill, still a bachelor and very much a man about town, went to a party given by Lady Granby, a famous beauty and the future Duchess of Rutland. The party was in the drawing room of her great town house in Arlington Street, close to the Court of St James and overlooking Green Park. The excited young minister was in search of a personal secretary to help him with his new governmental responsibilities. He discussed the matter with two of the older ladies present, first with his aunt Leonie, his mother's sister who was now Lady Leslie, and then with Lady Lytton, now the mother-in-law of the beautiful Pamela Plowden whom Churchill had once admired and unsuccessfully courted and who still remained his friend. Both these advisers encouraged Churchill to consider a young man who was present at the party that evening, a young civil servant and socialite named Edward Marsh. Looking across the room Churchill saw a somewhat foppish young man with a monocle, a long cigarette holder and a very high-pitched voice. Churchill recalled that he had met him very briefly a few weeks before at a country-house party. Churchill pondered the advice he had been given and the following morning decided to offer Marsh the job. Nervously, for he was in awe of Churchill's forceful personality, the 33-year-old aesthete and man of letters, some two years older than his new boss, accepted the offer.

Born into the middle class, of parents who had dedicated their lives to the swiftly developing hospital service of Victorian London, Edward Marsh had been sent to Trinity College, Cambridge, where he had a very successful academic career. As an undergraduate he was a regular contributor to the periodical *The Cambridge Observer*, which was run by his near contemporary Oswald Sickert, the younger brother of the eminent painter of that day. Edward Marsh contributed some considered reviews of the new works by established writers of the nineties such as Robert Louis Stevenson, Verlaine and Ibsen. He also came to know one of the most influential men of letters of the time, Edmund Gosse, and also the future poet laureate, Robert Bridges. At Trinity Marsh was a friend of his exact contemporary, Bertrand Russell, and of another Cambridge philosopher, G.E. Moore, whose influential *Principica Ethica* was published some three years before Edward Marsh began to work for Churchill. Moore's emphasis upon the value of art, feeling and friendship, rather than upon the heavy Victorian abstract nouns such as duty, honour and probity, was congenial to Marsh as it was to those other young Cambridge men who were just beginning to form what later would be known as the Bloomsbury Group. Edward Marsh was in fact close to several members of this set. He knew well the wealthy art critic Roger Fry, bought the work of the painter Duncan Grant and was a close friend of the novelist E.M. Forster. Edward Marsh shared not only Bloomsbury's thinking but also the homo-erotic feeling which so conspicuously characterised the group. He was strangely sexed. He was, reports his biographer, Christopher Hassall, who knew him well, 'incapable of the act of love'. He was, as the result of a boyhood illness, destined 'to live and die as chaste as the day he was born'. It is also the case that throughout his life Edward Marsh was a solicitous nurturer, patron and financial benefactor of handsome and gifted young men. The two chief objects of his devotion were the poet Rupert Brooke, who was to die in 1915, the year that proved traumatic for both Marsh and Churchill, and then Brooke's successor, Ivor Novello, the musical-comedy composer, performer, impresario and star who made his name as the author of one of the great hit songs of the First World War, 'Keep The Home Fires Burning'. A recent account of Novello's life, a life which comprised a succession of very active homosexual relationships from youth on, including one with Christopher Hassall, notes that Marsh was but 'a closet queen'. And the book shrinks from contemplating the possibility that Marsh might have served as a procurer in the sexual encounter between Churchill and Novello which Churchill in later life is said to have talked about to his friend the novelist Somerset Maugham. In this conversation reported by Maugham's long-time secretary and companion Alan Searle, Churchill denied rumours about homosexual involvements on his part in early life but spoke of the time he had a relationship with Novello just to find out 'what it would be like with a man'.

It seems most unlikely that Churchill did not know of Marsh's sexual interests and preferences. But his attitude to his loyal, thoroughly discreet, hard-working secretary was always worldly and indulgent. From early on in life Churchill had few illusions about people, at least about men. Such worldliness was a part of his sensibility. He had, for instance, a sexual sophistication far in advance of his fellow MPs in the Edwardian House of Commons, as was shown when early on in his career as a junior minister at the Colonial Office he had to defend to the House the use of 50,000 Chinese as indentured labourers herded together without women in the South African gold-fields. Speaking of the social conditions and the way of life of these workers, Churchill felt it necessary to speak of sodomy. The Speaker immediately felt it necessary to invite ladies to leave the visitors' gallery of the House. Churchill then informed the Radical questioner on his own back-benches that the evidence concerning unnatural vice was conflicting. The police found it very difficult to tell, just by looking at a Chinaman, whether he was a catamite or not. The word 'catamite', reported Edward Marsh in a letter full of characteristic giggle and sniff, was far too technical for Churchill's listeners. It 'was a great puzzle to the MPs, hardly anyone knew it'. Even the Hansard reporter thought that the word referred to some tribe in the Old Testament; 'in the proofs of the speech for Hansard Winston was made to say that it was very difficult to know by looking at the Chinamen whether or not they were Amalekites'. Winston, continued Marsh, shared his secretary's great amusement at his speech about 'sodomy among the Chinese' and was pleased to see himself described as some biblical figure who 'smote the Radicals hip and thigh from Sodom to Gomorrha'.

Churchill's worldliness in his bachelor days, reminiscent of that of a young Regency grandee, also showed itself, despite his usual shortage of money, in a very cavalier attitude to accumulating debt and to creditors. Less than a year after he had begun working for Churchill, Marsh was left behind in London to deal with all the duns while Churchill set off through France to Germany to observe the manoeuvres of the Kaiser's army at Breslau. From Paris Churchill wrote to Marsh telling him to fob off all the creditors as well as he could, confessing that 'I have been very wild out here and very dissipated'. Among his several costly purchases were 'a lot of nice French books'. When Edward Marsh later received the bills from two booksellers in Paris, he discovered that the books Churchill had bought amounted to 267 volumes. They covered French literature from the seventeenth century to the end of the nineteenth; they included *Manon Lescaut*, the *Correspondence of Louis XVI and Marie Antoinette* and the complete works of Maupassant, Balzac, Musset, Lamartine, Chateaubriand, Michelet, Madame de Sévigné and Voltaire. A taste for French books was one of the many literary sympathies shared by Churchill and his personal secretary. (Later in his life Edward Marsh was to devote himself to a well-received translation of the *Fables* of La Fontaine.) When, in September 1908, Churchill's bachelorhood came to an end and he married the 23-year-old Miss Clementine Hozier, who was some ten years younger than he, Edward Marsh's wedding present to them was the collected works of the French historian and literary critic Sainte-Beauve. Churchill was greatly touched and wrote a letter of thanks acknowledging a relationship that was more than that between an employer and an employee. 'Few people have been so lucky as me to find in the dull and grimy recesses of the Colonial Office a friend whom I shall cherish and hold to all my life. Yours always, W.' Churchill's confidence in the duration of the friendship was entirely justified. It would continue for some forty-five years and end only with the death of Edward Marsh a couple of months after his eightieth birthday, a loss which Churchill, then in his last term as Prime Minister, told *The Times* was 'a keen personal grief to me'.

Churchill's new bride took to Edward Marsh just as Churchill's mother, Lady Randolph, had done, despite her anxieties on Winston's behalf about the high-pitched voice. 'Eddie' became not just a friend but an intimate of the Churchills and their growing family, serving as godfather to their daughter, Sarah. A generous provider and supporter for so many other people, especially poets and painters, Eddie Marsh, in his own worst moments of illness, suffering and loneliness would invariably be received and tended and revitalised in the home of the Churchills.

One of the bonds between Churchill's bride, the famous Edwardian beauty Clementine Hozier, and Edward Marsh was they had both been close to the Sickert family. Clementine, like Winston, had an aristocratic background; she was a descendant of the Earls of Airlie. But, again like him, she went through the pains of growing up in aristocratic circles without the benefit of money or normal parental support. Her father and mother had separated and she and her mother and sisters continually moved from place to place, living in would-be genteel poverty. One of their longest residences was at Dieppe, the French coastal town favoured by many artists and writers at the turn of the century. Here it was that Clementine became well acquainted with the painter Walter Sickert. She also intrigued another resident of the town, George Du Maurier, the author of one of the most popular novels of the nineties, *Trilby*. Too characterful a girl to be susceptible to any hypnotising Svengali, Clementine returned to England and eked out a sparse living by giving French lessons to wealthy members of society. Something of a Cinderella figure who had to make her own clothes, Clementine had two uneasy engagements before marrying the moneyless but ambitious young politician and writer Winston Churchill. Her knowledge of France and of French culture and a lifelong Liberalism were some of the many gifts she brought to her husband in a long-enduring, if sometimes difficult, marriage.

About eighteen months after his wedding at St Margaret's, Westminster, the parish church of the House of Commons, Churchill was given yet one more grand promotion, this time to one of the great offices of state, that of Home Secretary. At thirty-five he was the youngest man ever to hold this position, with the one exception of the similarly and precociously brilliant Robert Peel, the creator of the first modern police force. The Liberal Prime Minister Henry Asquith entrusted Churchill with this office at a time when there was a good deal of social unrest in Britain. In 1909 Churchill's ministerial colleague the fiery Welsh Radical Lloyd George had, as Chancellor of the Exchequer, brought in the People's Budget. This involved what today seem rather innocuous taxes on the wealthy to pay for the expansion of the Royal Navy in the accelerating arms race with the Kaiser's Germany and for the Liberal programme of introducing old age pensions. The House of Lords angrily threw out the Budget and Asquith immediately called an election to allow the voters to decide between 'peers and people'. It was the final crisis of the aristocratic principle in British life. The Liberals were returned to office, though without an overall majority. Grudgingly the Lords passed the Budget, but then were confronted with a Parliament Bill which would abolish their right of veto and allow them only delaying powers over legislation passed by the Commons. Incensed, the Lords resisted. There was a bitter constitutional crisis. King Edward died in the midst of it. In August 1911 the new King, George V, was prevailed upon by the government to threaten the Tory Lords with the creation of enough Liberal peers to outvote them in the Upper House. The

Conservative peers finally backed down, the Parliament Bill went through and Britain took a major step towards full parliamentary democracy.

During these two and more years of political turbulence Churchill deployed all his very developed powers of oratory and rhetoric against the social class into which he had been born. And the Tories saved their most bitter anger for the man who had deserted their ranks. The Duke of Beaufort, for instance, a great hunting enthusiast, hoped to see Churchill and his upstart friend Lloyd George torn apart 'in the middle of twenty couple of dog-hounds'. For most Tories of that day found it impossible to understand why a man who had been born at Blenheim Palace, the grandson of a former Duke of Marlborough, and who was the good friend and frequent house guest of his cousin, the present Duke, and of many other aristocrats, should speak and write so powerfully for the destruction of the political power of his class. But the Liberal Churchill, powered in great part by his father's progressive feelings which, as a biographer, he had recently studied in such close detail, rode out and triumphed over the near fanatical Conservative animosity directed against him. The hatred accomplished nothing but it did not disappear. Within five years it would be given an opportunity to exact a harsh vengeance.

There were other acrimonious social divisions with which the new Home Secretary who presided over the ending of Edwardian England had to deal. The likely prospect of the Liberal government at last realising Gladstone's dream of passing a Home Rule bill for Ireland made protestant Ulster increasingly restive. Another campaign for political and constitutional reform, the suffragettes' demand for the vote for women, also brought about much disturbance and violence. Churchill was quick to improve the treatment of suffragettes in jail but he was not, to Clementine's regret, seen to be an unequivocal supporter of their cause. Some nine months after he became Home Secretary there occurred 'Black Friday', long remembered in the women's movement for the brutal treatment of suffragette demonstrators by the police. Along with other members of the Liberal government, Churchill was physically attacked by the feminists. In 1909 a woman had threatened to horsewhip him on the platform of the railway station at Bristol. Only intervention by Clementine had saved him from being knocked down in front of the wheels of an approaching train. After Black Friday a male supporter of the suffragettes cornered him in a train and tried to beat him up. Physically strong and ebullient, Churchill was not to be deterred by such attempts at violence. More painful and upsetting to him was the division which this issue created between him and his wife, who was a strong supporter of the women's cause.

The Edwardian decade ended also in an outburst of industrial unrest and violence. In the very months in which the Parliament Bill was made ready for the King's signature, a succession of strikes culminated in an extensive railway strike which brought with it widespread rioting. Churchill as Home Secretary, sensing society descending into chaos, sanctioned the sending of 50,000 troops to contain the strikes and to safeguard railway property. He organised resistance to the strikes like one conducting a military campaign. In the different riots six civilians were shot by the army. In the House of Commons Keir Hardie, who in 1892 had been the first ever Labour MP and who now represented the Welsh mining constituency of Merthyr Tydfil, denounced Churchill and protested passionately on behalf of the strikers who had been 'murdered by the government in the interests of the capitalist system'. It is clearly the case that, although Churchill was able to reach out imaginatively to the liberal middle class which in childhood he had been taught to regard as the political enemy, his sympathies never extended to the various working-class initiatives in politics and culture that developed in the new century both in Britain and abroad. At this time, even at his most liberal, he accepted as normal a virtually uncontrolled capitalist system and a conspicuously non-egalitarian social order. But he did not have the reactionary bloodlust that some subsequent left-wing mythologising has attributed to him. The events of 1911, the year in which the stability of the state was very much called into question, clearly created a panic in him. And this caused him to accept policies that led to actions going against his liberal view, stated in the House of Commons, that 'For soldiers to fire on the people would be a catastrophe in our national life'.

In the matter of industrial and class relationships Churchill's feelings and sensibility were much affected and informed by his literary studies and associations. Always an enthusiastic theatregoer (the theatre supplies many metaphors in his prose), Churchill had greatly admired John Galsworthy's play *Strife*, which was an outstanding success in the West End in 1909. A few years earlier Galsworthy had begun *The Forsyte Saga*, his long, popular sequence of novels criticising the philistinisms of the Victorian upper-middle class. The play *Strife*, which is in the fashionable realist mode of the time, takes up the subject of the contemporary industrial unrest. A paternalist director of a tin-plating works urges his fellow directors to give their workers a better deal. But the union leader with whom he is negotiating is called away when his wife dies as a result of the privations brought on by the strike. When he returns to the talks, the union leader finds that the kindly capitalist has been pushed aside and replaced by some of his fellow-directors who are thoroughgoing exploiters and gougers. These have enforced a harsh settlement upon the strikers while the union leader was absent. No very radical criticism of society, this play, so highly and widely admired at the time, deplores wicked capitalists and personalises, sentimentalises and applauds the workers' cause. *Strife* sees the removal of industrial confrontation as a matter not of structured or political change but of kindliness and decent human feeling. Galsworthy's liberalism mirrored that of many thousands of theatre-goers; very evidently it mirrored that of the Home Secretary too.

Churchill's under-secretary at the Home Office was C.F.G. Masterman, who was also a man of letters. The title of one of his books, *The Condition of England*, has long served as a label for a certain kind of English novel. Through Masterman Churchill came into social contact with Galsworthy. The two got on well. Throughout his political career Churchill was readily susceptible to and confirmed by the insights of his fellow men of letters. As *Strife* endorsed Churchill's perceptions of the industrial situation, so did Galsworthy's next theatrical success, *Justice*, inform Churchill's thinking about another of his responsibilities as Home Secretary, that of prison reform. The central character of this play is tried and imprisoned for altering the figure on a cheque. His defence council predicts how his client will be brutalised and reduced by the barbarities of the British prison system little more than a decade after Oscar Wilde was released from Reading Gaol. Harrowingly, somewhat pornographically, the play shows the humiliation and eventual destruction of the character, in great part as a result of his time in solitary confinement. The response of audiences was amazing. On the first night, the *Weekly Dispatch* reported, the members of the audience refused to leave the theatre at the end of the performance. Even after the management had darkened the theatre, they remained, 'calling for the author, shouting his name, singing it, shrieking out their determination to remain all night until he came forward'.

Churchill was immediately caught up in the reformist excitement generated by the play which was, reported Edward Marsh, 'the chief topic of conversation in all walks of life'. Writing to his close friend, the young poet Rupert Brooke, Churchill's secretary declared: 'I am tremendously for it, not having yet acquired enough Home Office *esprit de corps* to feel the resentment it inspires in my colleagues.' Marsh went with Winston and Clementine to see *Justice* on several occasions and the Home Secretary directed his secretary to write to the playwright telling how very much he 'looked forward to anything else he might write on the subject'. Lady Randolph Churchill gave a party in order to bring her son and the dramatist of the hour together again in an informal way. Once more the two talked together intensely and at great length and during the spring and summer of 1910 Galsworthy, the passionate libertarian, and Churchill, the Home Secretary, engaged in a lengthy and detailed correspondence on penal reform. And there can be no doubt that the progressive legislation which Churchill subsequently brought before the House of Commons owed a great deal to his association with this fellow-writer.

Ever receptive to the activities of the London theatre, Churchill also found himself for the first time, but by no means the last, involved with the new medium of film during the period of his tenure of the Home Office. This happened at another moment of great popular excitement, the so-called Siege of Sidney Street, at the beginning of that year of escalating political instability, panic and paranoia, 1911. Anarchists and nihilists and the atrocities of which they were capable were a great bogey in the minds of the Edwardians. They are, for example, the subject of a fine horror comedy of a novel of 1907, *The Secret Agent* by Masterman's friend, Joseph Conrad. In January 1911 a group of anarchists, refugees from Czarist Latvia, were cornered in a terraced house in Sidney Street, in the East End of London. The gang had earlier carried out a series of armed robberies in which they had killed three unarmed policemen. Churchill as Home Secretary sanctioned a police request to use the army – in the event, the Scots Guards and the Horse Artillery – to assist the police in the seemingly imminent gunfight with the terrorists. He himself went immediately to the scene. And when the house which was the anarchists' refuge was set on fire, Churchill took it upon himself to order the firemen not to risk their lives by attempting to put out the flames. When the fire eventually burned itself out two charred bodies were found in the building; one had been shot, the other was dead from asphyxiation. 'Peter the Painter', the supposed chief anarchist, was not found. A photograph of the episode shows Churchill with Edward Marsh behind him, both wearing the shiny silk top hats of the upper classes, watching events from immediately behind the armed soldiers. The episode was also one of the early ones to be recorded on newsreel film or what in 1911 was called 'the biograph'. 'I'm on the biograph,' proudly announced Edward Marsh to one of his many correspondents. 'I make a most gratifying appearance as almost the central figure of "Mr Churchill directing the operations".' But when he visited the Palace Theatre, the music hall or vaudeville where 'biographs' were shown, Marsh was dismayed to see himself received with 'unanimous boos and shouts of "shoot him" from the gallery'. 'Oh why,' wondered Eddie, 'are London music hall audiences so uniformly and so bigotedly Tory?'

The opposition in Parliament made much of what they regarded as Churchill's reckless, high-handed behaviour in the Sidney Street incident, conduct which necessitated his attendance at the inquest on the dead terrorists. The whole episode helped establish Churchill's reputation for aggressiveness and impetuosity, which was to affect his political career in later years. But Henry Asquith, the urbane Liberal Prime Minister, was impressed by Churchill's decisiveness and decided to employ him in Britain's ever more aggravated military rivalry with imperial Germany. In the same year as Sidney Street and the great constitutional and industrial crises in Britain, Europe as a whole had come close to war when the German navy had threatened French interests in the crisis of Agadir. (One reason for the Liberal government's panic about the railway strike was the widespread rumour that it was financed by 'German Gold' as part of a larger plan to cripple Britain's military mobility.) To ensure the most energetic defence of the country, in October Asquith asked Churchill to take over as First Lord of the Admiralty. He had been at the Home Office for only twenty months. The abruptness of the Cabinet shake-up was a measure of Asquith's anxiety about German intentions. At that time the Royal Navy was the pre-eminent part of the defence of Great Britain. Not just the senior service, it was by far the largest navy in the world and accepted, even by former soldiers such as Churchill, as much more important than the army in the defence of Britain and the far-flung British Empire.

With characteristic drive Churchill set about the reforms he judged necessary to make the Navy ready for the war which increasingly he sensed to be imminent. He took the dangerous risk of choosing Sir John Fisher, a geriatric, vindictive, but at times hyper-energetic and innovative martinet, as his First Sea Lord. He arranged for the biggest-ever guns to be installed in British battleships. He founded the Royal Navy Air Service, which was later to evolve into the RAF. He took the decision that the Navy's great combat vessels should no longer be powered by coal but by oil. This entailed a deal with the Anglo-Persian oil company and substantial governmental investment in its oilfields. One of the many historical decisions which Churchill took during his lifetime, this began a new and fateful British involvement in the Middle East.

Running the Admiralty was a challenge to Churchill's capacity for hard work, one which, as usual, he impressively met. But the job also brought with it what was for Churchill an especially enjoyable reward in the form of access at any time to the very luxurious steam yacht HMS *Enchantress*, which was one of the perks of the First Lord of the Admiralty. Churchill came to love this beautiful ship. He spent so much time on it that questions were asked in the House of Commons. One member pointed out that Churchill could visit naval bases in Scotland far more cheaply by travelling first class on the train than by embarking on the *Enchantress* and sailing up the North Sea. In the summer of 1913, that last year before the Great War changed the entire world order, Churchill set off on the *Enchantress* for the Mediterranean, ostensibly to discuss with the British commander in Egypt (whom he had severely criticised in *The River War*), Horatio Herbert Kitchener, the right balance of British sea power between the Mediterranean and the North Sea. Churchill and his wife were accompanied by the Prime Minister and Mrs Asquith and Asquith's lively daughter, Violet, who, like Churchill, shared the literary interests of Edward Marsh who sailed with them. They steamed leisurely down to Gibraltar, across to Sicily and up to Venice for a few days. Slowly they returned down the Adriatic and anchored for a time off Albania, where Winston organised some seine fishing. They caught a few fish and had a picnic on the beautiful unspoiled coast that Byron had known. The late May weather was superb and Winston, to articulate this pleasure and to indulge his own enthusiasm for declaiming poetry, kept reciting Gray's 'Ode To Spring', with great emphasis upon the words 'At ease reclined in rustic state'. (Some years before, in order to entertain the companionable Violet Asquith, Churchill had learned to recite all of the *Odes* of Keats.)

When they arrived in a very hot Athens, the distinguished British party went to view the Pantheon. Winston was irritated to see the ancient tumbled columns lying around and suggested that a party of the hundred bluejackets who crewed the *Enchantress* might be detailed to set them up again. But the Greeks politely declined his offered help. When the happy travellers arrived again off Sicily the Prime Minister, like Gladstone before him, an accomplished classical scholar, supplied the party with a lucid, entertaining account of the Sicilian Expedition as related by Thucydides. And from the stage of the Greek theatre at Syracuse Eddie Marsh declaimed a camp parody of a Greek tragedy. 'It was a wonder,' he remarked later, with one of his shrill laughs, 'that the offended shade of Aeschylus didn't send an eagle to drop a tortoise on my head.'

Just a year earlier Edward Marsh had committed himself to a more serious literary enterprise, the compilation and publication of a collection of poems by new young writers. It was called *The Georgian Anthology* and the title intimated the new modes of feeling and expression which Marsh believed to be emerging at the same time as the new reign. Marsh published a sequence of such anthologies during the early years of George V's reign and they were very successful. The poems chosen had none of the rhetoric, abstraction and clanking rhythms and rhymes of Kipling and Chesterton. They were in great part pastoral and reflective. Not so radical a challenge to late Victorian poetry as Ezra Pound's collection *Des Imagistes*, published at about the same time, Marsh's sequence of anthologies did contain the work of important modernist writers such as D.H. Lawrence and James Joyce. Through Marsh and his publishing activities Churchill had yet another contact with, and access to, the literary world of the day. In a few years' time a great conflict in Churchill's mind would be acted out in a meeting with one of Marsh's authors, Siegfried Sassoon, a Georgian sensibility ravaged by the horrors of the trench fighting in the Great War.

But during that happy Mediterranean cruise in 1913 such horrors were still unimagined. Having sailed northwest from Sicily the *Enchantress* docked at Ajaccio, in Corsica, where Churchill, accompanied by Edward Marsh, went to the house of Napoleon, a figure who fascinated Churchill throughout his life. In the upstairs room he stood 'for a full minute in silent cogitation'. Then the party sailed on to Gibraltar and thence to Southampton, and that last full, leisurely summer of the *ancien regime* drew to an end.

II

In the next session of Parliament and on through into 1914, as the larger European situation became ever more dangerous, defence preoccupied the House of Commons. Churchill as First Lord became involved in the ongoing confrontation about the naval estimates with the Chancellor of the Exchequer, his Welsh friend, the wiley David Lloyd George. Ireland too was an important concern as Parliament moved ever closer to a solution of the complicated problem of the six counties of Ulster. A dramatic passage in Churchill's reminiscences of this suspenseful time recalls how at a meeting of the Cabinet, struggling with the final resolution of the complexities 'of the borders and the muddy byways of Fermanagh and Tyrone', members suddenly became aware of the Foreign Secretary, Sir Edward Grey, making himself heard as he read out the details of the ultimatum which the Austro-Hungarian Empire had delivered to Serbia following the assassination of the Austrian Archduke Francis Ferdinand. This was the beginning of the end of peace. When Russia went to the aid of the

UNDER HIS MASTER'S EYE

Scene—Mediterranean, on board the Admiralty yacht, " Enchantress".

A Punch *cartoon of Churchill as First Lord of the Admiralty holidaying with the Prime Minister on board H.M.S.* Enchantress *in the Mediterranean. The cartoonist satirises Churchill's egotism by showing his reading to be his own most recent book, here incorrectly titled* My Journey In Africa.

Serbs, their fellow Slavs, Germany declared war on the Russians and their ally, France. Germany also invaded neutral Belgium. The strong anti-war element in Britain's Liberal government, whose most eloquent spokesman was the radical Lloyd George, was impressed by the desperate appeal from the King of the Belgians even more than by British commitments to France and Russia. Within ten days of the ultimatum that so shocked the Cabinet, Britain, with only a small number of Liberal cabinet ministers resigning, went to war. In practical terms it began when Churchill, at the Admiralty, signalled to the Fleet: 'Commence hostilities against Germany.'

By early 1915 the ground war in France had settled down into that horrific, obscene yet futile trench war that over the next three years was to cost millions of lives. In the early naval war Britain was for the most part in control of the seas, but did suffer some embarrassing reverses such as the sinking of some British ships off Coronal in the South Pacific by the German Pacific Squadron. This was avenged a month later in a battle in the South Atlantic off the Falkland Islands. But the original defeat harmed Churchill's political standing as the First Lord. The so-called Antwerp episode did still more damage. When the Germans were about to capture this strategically important port in Belgium, Churchill himself left the Admiralty and hurried off to direct his marines in defending the city. He became emotionally involved in the fighting and went so far as to ask the Prime Minister to relieve him of his responsibilities as First Lord and to let him devote himself entirely to the defence of Antwerp. Violet Asquith, ever sympathetic to her friend Winston, but also politically shrewd, remarked of this request that it was 'the choice of a romantic child'. The Cabinet ministers laughed heartily as they supported Asquith in refusing Churchill's resignation. Churchill himself, writing about the Antwerp episode in his next book, defended himself against 'the reproaches and foolish fictions which have been so long freely and ignorantly heaped upon me'. But he went on to concede that, 'No doubt had I been ten years older, I should have hesitated long before accepting so unpromising a task.'

But much worse was to happen, and quickly, to detract from Churchill's once impressive political credibility. Horrified by the heavy losses and the lack of any progress on the western front in France, Churchill was one of those who advocated attacking Germany and the Austrian Empire from the east. They and their ally Turkey could be seriously weakened by an invasion of Eastern Europe through the Dardanelles. Such an attack would also take the pressure off hard-pressed Czarist Russia. Plans were made to force the straits of the Dardanelles by the Royal Navy, assisted by vessels from the French fleet. When the operation began the admirals in charge encountered unexpected minefields and declined to risk their ships by advancing any further. A land attack was then mounted on the straits at Gallipoli by troops mainly from Australia and New Zealand. But this landing was repelled by the Turks and the words Gallipoli and Dardanelles became synonyms for disaster.

The utter failure of this eastern initiative was a main reason for the break-up of Asquith's Liberal government. Experiencing great unpopularity and a lack of confidence, the Prime Minister felt compelled to turn to the Conservatives for help in forming a new coalition government. Part of the price demanded by the Conservatives for their joining with Asquith was the exclusion from any major office of Winston Churchill. Their moment of vengeance had come. The man whom they had long hated as a renegade they now denounced as a political and administrative failure. They insisted, successfully, on his complete exclusion from governmental decision-making. Asquith did his best to soften the blow for his senior colleague and managed to retain a seat in the Cabinet for him with a sinecure of a job as Chancellor of the Duchy of Lancaster. But, for Churchill, this demotion into virtual obscurity was a painful humiliation. He endured it only a few months before tendering his resignation. The only honourable course that he could see open to him was to set off for France with the rank of major (which he had acquired as a territorial soldier in the Oxfordshire Yeomanry), to take his place in the trenches.

With his dismissal from power Churchill lost his handsome eighteenth-century residence at Admiralty House in Whitehall. He also lost his salary, for though in those days Ministers received salaries, MPs did not. Suddenly without a home and without an income, Winston and Clementine were compelled to move in with his younger brother Jack and his wife Goonie, the daughter of the Earl of Abingdon, in their rented house, number 41, Cromwell Road.

It was here on 14 November 1915 that Churchill in very straitened circumstances gave a farewell lunch for those closest to him. Among those who came to commiserate with Winston and Clementine were Eddie Marsh, Margot Asquith, the Prime Minister's wife, and his daughter Violet. Violet later described the suppressed misery at the lunch. 'Clemmie was admirably calm and brave, poor Eddie blinking back his tears, the rest of us trying to "play up" and hide our leaden hearts.' 'For most of us it was a kind of wake', even though Winston made a point of being 'at his gayest and best'. With all his own troubles Winston found time to make provision for his private secretary, 'as he could not bear to think of poor Eddie Marsh being plunged back into the bowels of the Colonial Office, sans personal function, sans friends, sans anything. So he was coming to us at No.10 to be put in charge of Civil List Pensions which we hoped would make him feel a little less of a motherless child.' One of Edward Marsh's actions while doing this job in Downing Street was to be of note in literary history; in association with Ezra Pound and W.B. Yeats, he arranged a civil list pension for the little-known writer James Joyce.

The day after that tense lunch at 41 Cromwell Road, Max Aitken, Lord Beaverbrook, the Canadian tycoon and newspaper proprietor, called at the house, to find Churchill packing. In his book of reminiscences, *Politicians and the War*, he later described with some puckish irony how 'the whole household was upside down while the soldier statesman was buckling on his sword'. 'Downstairs, Mr Eddie Marsh . . . was in tears . . . Upstairs, Lady Randolph was in a state of despair at the idea of her brilliant son being relegated to the trenches. Mrs Churchill seemed to be the only person who remained calm, collected and efficient.' The following day Britain's former chief warlord, now but an officer of quite junior rank, crossed over to France to report for duty. The swiftly, dazzlingly successful political career was seemingly at an end.

Within but a few months the power and eminence he had acquired during some ten years of office was completely gone from him. The Dardanelles and his abrupt, sickening descent into failure constituted without doubt the most traumatic experience of Churchill's adult life so far. At the age of forty he was suddenly no longer who he had been. No longer a leading statesman, a minister or even a functioning politician, he was an outcast and a failure.

During the war decade of the 1910s Churchill was too much taken up with events to write very much. But when the Great War at last exhausted itself, Churchill immediately set about writing his account of the events which had halted his life progress and completely destroyed the social and political order in which he had grown up. And at the centre of this story, and ever recurring within it, is his preoccupation as man and writer with the failure at the Dardanelles, the failure that called into question his entire career and his sense and definition of himself. The story of this simultaneously personal and historic catastrophe he entitled *The World Crisis*. It is a vast work of four volumes and some 2,500 pages. It is a work of history and reflection, scholarship and polemic, humour and anger. Above all it is an instance of one of the great prose forms, the apologia. It is the justification of a selfhood by one that has known that selfhood impugned and declared to be a redundancy and a failure.

CHAPTER FIVE

The Apologist

I

For well over a year and a half, from November 1915 until July 1917, Churchill, who for over ten years had seen more and still more power accrue to him, was entirely excluded from power. He was, as his daughter Mary Soames has written, 'politically down-and-out'. His letters to Clementine from the front, where he had become a colonel in the 6th Battalion of the Royal Scots Fusiliers, show how distraught he was at his ostracism and exile. He was obsessed with the question of how he might most speedily renew his career at Westminster. He was avid for the slightest crumb of political information that Clementine could find for him in London, and he urged her to go to social gatherings in governmental circles to find out what she could for him. She had to put up with many a snub, but she agreed to accept social invitations from the Asquiths and 'to put my pride in my pocket and reconnoitre Downing Street'.

Her letters to Winston during this unhappy time show not only her intense love for him but also her detailed political knowledge and her canniness. She read the minutest changes in the mood of the government acutely, despite her feelings of resentment and distaste towards its members. 'The Government people are unbelievably smug – I am seeing them occasionally to please you my Darling but I cannot take any interest in these soul-less cold-blooded tortoises . . .' Occasionally Clementine despaired; with one tired, sad letter she enclosed a copy in her own handwriting of Christina Rossetti's poem of demoralisation and weariness, 'Up-Hill', beginning with the lines 'Does the road wind up-hill all the way?/ Yes, to the very end.' But despite such occasional depression she stuck to her political task on Winston's behalf, always encouraging him, 'Do not fear, your political estate has not vanished, it is all waiting for you when the right moment comes . . . If only you come safely thro' . . .' Always afraid of what she might learn of Winston's fate in the fighting zone, Clementine was a little relieved when for military headgear he exchanged the cloth glengarry of the Royal Scots Fusiliers for the pointed steel helmet of the French infantry – the *poilus*.

In her political reports to her husband, Clementine's greatest dislike was reserved for Winston's ten-year political associate and friend, Lloyd George. Quite often they disagreed profoundly on their judgements of people. To some, Lloyd George was the Welsh Wizard or, as Winston was to say years later, 'the greatest Welshman since the Tudors'. To others he was 'the Goat', so called because of his long hair and formidable sexual appetites and agility. To such observers the sexual acrobatics were a perfect image of his political ones. To the rather staid Clementine Churchill, fanatically and shrewdly jealous of her husband's interests, Lloyd George was treachery personified. 'I assure you he is the direct descendant of Judas Iscariott [sic].' Were it to be socially necessary to shake his hand, 'I would have to safeguard myself with charms, touchwoods, exorcisms and by crossing myself . . .'

And yet it was Lloyd George who, some time after he had displaced Asquith as Prime Minister, in 1917 was at last able to bring Churchill back into government, though not by any means in the kind of exalted office to which he had been accustomed. With the grudging consent of the Tory members of the coalition, Lloyd George invited Churchill to become his Minister of Munitions in the last gruelling year of the Great War. With immense relief and gratitude to Lloyd George for this 'fresh horse', Churchill duly established himself not in an elegant Whitehall building but in the requisitioned Hotel Metropole, in Northumberland Avenue, not too far from Trafalgar Square, which had been taken over by the government as the home for the recently created Ministry of Munitions.

Equally suddenly Churchill found that he had a French chateau at his disposal. His new job required a good deal of liaison with commanders in the field and this meant a French headquarters. He was given the use of the Chateau Verchocq, to which he travelled by air regularly. His room there, he told Clementine in a letter, was 'charming', 'filled with a sort of ancient wood-carved furniture that you admire and which seems to me to be very fine and old. The grounds contain avenues of the most beautiful trees, beech and pine, grown to an enormous height and making broad walks like the aisles of cathedrals. One of these must be nearly half a mile long.' In these congenial surroundings, not far from where he had recently served in the trenches, Churchill worked away with a will and with characteristic energy to make the badly needed improvements in the provisioning of the troops. But as he worked, he became more and more obsessed with one of the most highly publicised anti-war protesters. This was the poet Siegfried Sassoon.

One evening at the Chateau, Churchill and his staff and several senior officers had a convivial dinner together. The meal came to a pleasing conclusion but the drinking long continued. Then Churchill's very relaxed companions were suddenly astonished to hear Churchill declaiming from memory and with passion poems that were bitterly critical of the British government and its generals and senior officers. The poems were from Siegfried Sassoon's recently published volume, *Counter Attack*.

Sassoon was an intense, nervy young man who had been educated at Marlborough and Clare College, Cambridge. His father was from a wealthy Jewish family; one of his mother's brothers was a successful artist in Victorian Kensington. Siegfried had grown up in Kent, where he had developed a taste for hunting and for horses. A rather moony literary dilettante, he also cultivated the style of a country squire. When war came in 1914, he quickly enlisted and served as a lieutenant in the Royal Welsh Fusiliers, where he became friendly with another poet, Robert Graves, the future author of a classic account of the warfare on the western front, *Goodbye To All That*. Sassoon became well known for his personal courage and in 1916 was awarded the Military Cross for his fearlessness in bringing back to the British trenches comrades who had been wounded in an attack on Mametz wood. As the trench warfare grew ever more destructive and obscene, Sassoon's poetry developed a realism to match the ever increasing horror and its psychological effects.

Do you remember the dark months you held the sector at Mametz, –
The nights you watched and wired and dug and piled sandbags on parapets?
Do you remember the rats; and the stench
Of corpses rotting in front of the front-line trench, –
And dawn coming, dirty white, and chill . . .
The rank stench of those bodies haunts me still.
And I remember things I'd best forget.

Sassoon grew more and more psychologically distressed and was invalided back to England to recuperate. When requested to rejoin his battalion near Liverpool, he took with him his Military Cross and hurled it into the River Mersey. He then went on to make another act of protest against the war, an act which caused considerable political commotion in Britain. On 6 July 1917 there appeared in *The Times* a statement signed by Sassoon, the opening sentence of which proclaimed the statement to be 'an act of wilful defiance of military authority'. The declaration, which was read out in the House of Commons, also contained the sentence, 'I have seen and endured the sufferings of the troops, and I can no longer be a party to prolong these sufferings for ends which I believe to be evil and unjust.'

Sassoon hoped for a court martial to bring still more publicity to his protest. But his friend Robert Graves sought to persuade him to agree to the Army's request that he attend a medical board. Graves feared for his friend's sanity when Sassoon told him of how he saw decomposing corpses of soldiers lying about him as he walked in the streets of Liverpool. Robert Graves was also very sceptical about the way in which Bertrand Russell and other leading members of the pacifist cause were using his tormented friend in order to further their aims. In the event, Sassoon attended a medical board, which sent him to a hospital for shell-shocked officers at Craiglockhart, near Edinburgh. A fellow-patient there was the greatest of the British poets of the First World War, Wilfred Owen.

But Sassoon's protest was an important marker of the intensifying disillusion with the war. It clearly had a considerable impact on Winston Churchill, himself not long since a soldier in the trenches, who went and bought Sassoon's books, read them and memorised his poems. Late one summer night, under the ornate gleaming chandelier in the grand dining room at the Chateau Verchocq, as the senior officers and War office officials relaxed and sprawled over their port and brandy, Siegfried Sassoon's feelings came pouring out in Winston Churchill's voice.

Twenty-seven-year-old Lieutenant Gilbert Hall of the Royal Flying Corps was Churchill's personal pilot; he flew the two-seater bi-plane which transported the Minister of Munitions from the Kent suburbs of London to northern France. He was present at the chateau on that night of late drinking and long remembered the consternation that was caused by Churchill's lengthy sequence of recitations from Sassoon. Some of his listeners murmured and then loudly protested that Sassoon's poems about the foul misery and the futility of war were unpatriotic. If they became well known, they would damage the morale of the troops and discourage badly needed recruits. Sassoon was a dangerous and subversive man. But Churchill rounded on these objectors and silenced them. He loudly declared his admiration for Sassoon as a man, as a soldier and as a poet. Truculently he declared that, despite what he had heard that night, he would, when he returned to England, make a point of getting in touch with Sassoon and try to make him some amends, possibly by finding him a job in the Ministry of Munitions. Lieutenant Hall then remembered Major Jack Churchill, always concerned for his elder brother's political wellbeing, shouting out: 'I should leave that man alone if I were you. He might start writing a poem about you.' Winston looked his uniformed brother in the eye and said, slowly and confidently, 'I am not a bit afraid of Siegfried Sassoon. That man can think. I am afraid only of people who cannot think.'

When he returned to London Churchill was as good as his word in arranging a meeting with Sassoon. Knowing that Eddie Marsh was acquainted with Sassoon, as with so many contemporary poets, Churchill asked if he would try to get him to come and see him. Marsh persuaded the poet to come up to London, put him up in his own rooms in Gray's Inn, and took him round to see Churchill in his makeshift office in the Hotel Metropole. The meeting between the two men was marked by a duality, a schizophrenia even, in Churchill's behaviour such as was also to inform his attitude to the war in his vast apologia *The World Crisis*.

In his volume of autobiography, *Siegfried's Journey* – like Churchill's *My Early Life*, one of the important instances of this particular prose form in this century – Sassoon describes the meeting. It began amicably with a beaming, conspicuously relaxed Churchill putting the shy young poet, twelve years his junior, at his ease. They talked about their shared interest in horses and in hunting. Churchill lit a cigar, leaned back in his chair and reminisced about another poet who was a friend of his, the fiery Victorian radical Wilfred Scawen Blunt, who had once been jailed for two months for his zealous efforts on behalf of Irish Home Rule. He spoke of 'the memorable quality' of Sassoon's war poems and then gradually broached the subject of his visitor's attitudes to the war. The somewhat gangling young man spoke up strongly but not, he later thought, sufficiently eloquently, for his deeply held beliefs. He felt that the thick-set, balding minister had a compulsion 'to have it out' with him. Nevertheless there was also a strong sympathy there, a 'candid geniality' which, Sassoon recalled, made 'me feel that I should like to have him as my company commander in the front line'.

But then, abruptly, Churchill's mood changed. He stood up, thrust back his chair noisily and started pacing about the dusty hotel sitting room. Up and down he marched, his hands clasped behind his back, the cigar stuck in the corner of his mouth, all the time speaking of war as an important and necessary part of life, a way of advancing science, the greatest of opportunities for a man to test and to realise himself. Sometimes the heavy, insistent figure bore down upon the dark, thin-faced poet until he stood just inches away from him, his urgent words booming and resounding. Sassoon was given no chance to reply. Just for a moment Churchill paused to puff on his cigar and assure his guest of a job in the Ministry of Munitions. Then Churchill was back to his harangue, with its aggressive body language. Edward Marsh suddenly tapped at the door, put his head round and announced a new visitor. Churchill irritably waved him away and continued his monologue to Sassoon. Five minutes later a nervous Edward Marsh tried again. Churchill slowed down, then reluctantly fell silent. Sassoon rose and the two men shook hands awkwardly. The meeting was over.

Churchill's violent mood swing on this occasion has its counterpart in the style of *The World Crisis*. There was a nagging, painful conflict in his mind between, on the one hand, certain Victorian phrases with which he had grown up and which he continued to honour such as 'soldierly duty', 'moral and physical endurance', 'courage' and 'the art of war' and, on the other hand, the terrible images of combat in the present war which he, a soldier and correspondent in at least three other campaigns, had found unprecedentedly horrific. At times in his apologia the writing is that of someone seeking to suppress the latter perceptions in order to safeguard, or, at least, not to abandon, the former assumptions. It is also abundantly clear that Churchill's commitment to fighting the war somewhere besides France, to the attack on the Dardanelles, the central subject of the dramatic second volume, was inspired by that same horror of the trenches of the Western Front which deep down, but obviously uneasily, Churchill shared with Siegfried Sassoon.

II

When the war finally ended, Lloyd George was quick to call a general election, with popular promises to 'hang the Kaiser' and to squeeze the Germans 'until the pips squeak'. The Welsh Wizard, who was also proclaimed 'the man who won the war' with his coalition of Conservatives and fewer Liberals, won the election and Churchill, who had been an effective Minister of Munitions, was promoted to become Minister of War. As he worked at the complex problem of demobilising the armed forces and at the issues created by the ongoing peace negotiations at Versailles, Churchill in 1919 devoted virtually every minute of his spare time to the writing of his apologia.

At the end of the year there appeared the final report of the Dardanelles Commission, which had been appointed to investigate the causes of that colossal political and military disaster. The venture was judged to be a correct one in principle and Churchill was not personally censured for his central part in it. But the report did revive a great deal of controversy and recrimination and Churchill became impatient to have his account of the debacle and of the larger course of the war appear in print. Sensing the interest his story would be likely to have in the United States, Churchill entered into an arrangement with the American literary agency Curtis Brown for the selling of his projected book. Curtis Brown also did well on his behalf in Britain. They obtained a large advance from the London publishing house of Thornton Butterworth and they sold the serialisation rights to *The Times*. In the United States the book was placed with Scribner's, the then eighty-year-old publishing house which was currently adding to its list two other younger writers who in differing ways dealt with the subject of the recent war, Scott Fitzgerald and Ernest Hemingway. As his first advance payment, Churchill received from Scribner's a cheque for £3,000. Though always plagued with debt and with other money problems, Churchill went out and spent all but a few hundred pounds of this money on a new Rolls-Royce.

In February of 1921 Lloyd George transferred Churchill from the War Office to the Colonial Office. This new job brought with it some difficult, near insoluble problems. As Colonial Secretary at this time Churchill was the maker of political arrangements that were to continue problematical for the rest of the century. He was the minister who pushed through Parliament the bill granting Home Rule to Ireland, with a partitioned Ulster. He also presided over the dividing up of that part of the old Turkish Empire that had been mandated to Britain and he was, therefore, responsible for the creation of such problem states of the future as Palestine, Jordan and Iraq. In his thinking about the complexities of Arab politics, Churchill was assisted by one of the great heroes of the First World War and a then very highly regarded man of letters, the author of *The Seven Pillars of Wisdom*, Colonel T.E. Lawrence. In later years, when Churchill the writer turned once more to fine-tuning the essay form, one of his achievements in this prose genre was, as we shall see, his 'Lawrence of Arabia'.

In this same year, as he struggled with so many intractable political problems, Churchill was hammered by personal tragedies. That summer his mother, Lady Randolph, still a socialite and a literary dilettante, a woman in her mid-sixties now married to a third husband in his early forties, fell down a staircase at the eighteenth-century mansion of Mells Park in Somerset. The accident occurred because she was wearing fashionable high heels for a ball. She seriously injured her leg. Gangrene set in and, to save her life, her leg was amputated. The operation was not a cure. After much agony Lady Randolph died of a major haemorrhage. Then, in less than two months, the Churchills' youngest child Marigold developed a raging throat infection which the doctors in that age before antibiotics were unable to control. Two years and nine months old, the little girl died painfully while her parents looked helplessly on. Winston long remembered how 'Clementine in her agony gave a succession of wild shrieks, like an animal in mortal pain'.

Losing a mother and a daughter within weeks of each other, and overwhelmed with work, Churchill was understandably in an extreme psychological state at this time. One way in which it found expression was in the intemperance and near hysteria of the language with which he denounced Lenin and the Russian government, which by now was clearly establishing itself as the replacement of that of the Czars. Yet, for all his upset, Churchill worked hard at his book whenever he could. On Boxing Day of 1921 he set off for the South of France to write and spend the New Year's holiday in Cannes, at the sumptuous home of the Countess of Essex. (Too weak to travel, Clementine, in London, found herself having to take care of a houseful of children coming down with the Spanish influenza.) Setting out from the Gare D'Orsay in Paris, Churchill had Lloyd George as a companion in his first-class compartment. In the train heading south through France, the Prime Minister read some of the chapters and, so Churchill wrote to his wife, 'praised the style and made several pregnant suggestions [which] I am embodying'. Able to make swifter progress with the writing, Churchill grew excited about the book, seeing it yet again as a great 'chance to put my whole case'. At Cannes, comfortably close to the gambling casinos, which he never could resist, Churchill submitted his manuscript to another of the house guests, a writer of aristocratic background, Evan Charteris, the biographer of the painter John Singer Sargent and a trustee of the Tate Gallery and the National Gallery, and also, in the recent war, a captain in the Royal Flying Corps and the Tank Corps. Increasingly as his career as a writer developed, Churchill would show the current work in progress to others. In his latter years Churchill's authorship would become difficult to separate from group authorship.

III

That New Year of 1922 was to give a great boost to Churchill's activities as a writer. Suddenly, disconcertingly, he was able to devote all his time to *The World Crisis*. For the Conservatives withdrew from Lloyd George's coalition government, a General Election was held and Churchill was defeated in his constituency of Dundee. He was again, perforce, a full-time writer. The year 1922 was a historical year in British life and culture. It was the year of *The Waste Land* in poetry and of *Ulysses* in fiction. It was the year that began the permanent marginalisation of the Liberal party to which Churchill belonged. It would never be either the government or the chief and united opposition party again. As the latter, its place was taken by the Labour party. As a Lloyd George Liberal, Churchill was to be politically homeless for nigh on a couple of years. Ill and demoralised after his defeat, Churchill again set off for the South of France, where he recuperated for some six months, working all the time to complete his book, with occasional research trips back to London, where he worked at the Ritz Hotel in Piccadilly. At long, long last the first volume of *The World Crisis* appeared in book form in April 1923.

The somewhat effeminate Arthur Balfour, who had been the friend of Winston's father in Tory Democracy days and who had gone on to become Prime Minister early in the Edwardian decade, was seventy-five years old when *The World Crisis* first appeared. He described it as 'a brilliant autobiography disguised as a history of the universe'. Indeed, Churchill's apologia has a grand historical resonance to it. The first two chapters, which form a prelude, have epigraphs from a Latin and a Greek prose writer which proclaim Churchill's view of his story as having an importance comparable to that of those told by the classic narrators of the origins of Western experience. Brought up at Harrow on the classics, then, more importantly, self-educated in the classics, Churchill uses Greece and Rome as recurrent markers as, throughout the decade of the 1920s, he adds volume to volume about what he saw as simultaneously a personal crisis and a crisis of the West. In the very first chapter he cites Herodotus as, in summarising the prelude years 1870–1904, he sets out 'to put on record what were their grounds of feud'. And as he proceeds to look back upon and to describe the convert hostilities that festered in Europe between 1905 and 1910, his view is encapsulated in a sentence from Cicero: 'Enmities which are unspoken and hidden are more to be feared than those which are spoken and open.'

A mental gap exists between Churchill and readers of today since he did not try to understand the devastating crisis of his times by recourse to economic forces, consumer possibilities, sociology or the various forms of political science. Child of the Victorian age that he was, Churchill looked to something called history, a process of which the Greeks and the Romans were the great and the founding exemplars. But, and this is one of the many complexities of his mind, he was also very much a man of the twentieth century, sharing its characteristic interests in, to take just one instance, the possibilities of technology. He prides himself, for example, on his part in the development of the tank. The historian so mindful of the classics writes also as the futurologist. He remembers how as First Lord, in charge of the Royal Marines, he had been a member of what the Admiralty, inventing a new word, had called its 'Landships Committee'. The 'landship', even as the Germans dug trenches to defend their captured land, was still an image of fantasy. 'Mr H.G. Wells', recalls Churchill, 'in an article written in 1903, had practically exhausted the possibilities of imagination in this sphere.' But bit by bit the fabulous 'landship' became actualised in the 'tank'. He concedes: 'There never was a person about whom it could be said "this man invented the tank". But there was a moment when the actual manufacture of the first tanks was definitely ordered.' And Churchill claims responsibility for that historic order. 'I was prepared to incur both risk and responsibility in providing the necessary funds and in issuing the necessary authority.' It was a moment of pride for the historian when the first of these unprecedented, unimaginable, outlandish machines was finally put on display outside Lord Salisbury's great Tudor mansion at Hatfield in January 1916.

The accounts of such political – or, rather, bureaucratic – achievements are, in context, but lengthy asides from the slow, measured prelude which the early chapters comprise. For the most part the chapters in this, the quietest of the volumes, are sedate, systematic, Augustan. Just occasionally the writing works itself up into a prose poem, as when Churchill looks back and contemplates the great assembly of the Royal Navy in the spring of 1912 and, imaginatively putting himself back into that time, envisions with a Wellsian sense of future horror what would happen to the world if all the seacocks were opened and all these great vessels, which ruled the waves, were scuttled. Also, on occasion, the measured pace of the prose is interrupted by one of those succinct characterisations of someone which constitute one of Churchill's special literary skills. The old, mongol-faced prima donna of an admiral, Lord Fisher, was one of the daemons of Churchill's life. Churchill admired him and yet was greatly damaged by him. His last of many petulant resignations helped precipitate Churchill's downfall in 1915, yet Churchill's continuing fascination with him still lives in a handful of words and a concept derived most immediately from George Bernard Shaw. Fisher was a man who 'hurled himself into . . . business with explosive energy'. 'He was far more often right than wrong and his drive and life-force made the Admiralty quiver like one of his great ships at its highest speed.'

The first volume ends with the beginning of the stalemate brought about by the consolidation of the trench war in France in early 1915. 'Shall our armies toil only in the mud of Flanders or shall we break new ground?' So demands Churchill in one of a sequence of rhetorical questions which build operatically to a crescendo. To his first readers in the 1920s these concluding paragraphs would have had some suspense to them. For they are a rhetorical device preparing the way for that 'new ground', that great climax of the war and the author's personal nadir, the Dardanelles.

The title of the second volume, *The World Crisis 1915*, spotlights the terrible year. Churchill, as he datelines his preface, 13 August 1923, also gives the reader notice of a clear-cut change of attitude and tone in the writing. 'I must . . . at the outset,' he announces, 'disclaim the position of historian.' 'Upon me more than any other person the responsibility for the Dardanelles and all that it involved has been cast.' His intention is to make his apologia 'without bitterness'. But in writing of such painful memories it is not easy to employ what, in a rich seven-word phrase, he calls 'the easily turned language of the aftertime'. For Churchill, eight years on, the Dardanelles is still too present, too vivid to be an 'aftertime'. In remembering, reliving and describing those times, 'I expose myself to an ordeal.'

The book opens with a powerful prose poem about the surreal experience of being carried along ever more swiftly by a crazy, disastrous process of international war which neither individuals nor governments know how to halt. This was the appalling group insanity which Churchill remembered from early 1915 as 'Governments and individuals conformed to the rhythm of the tragedy, and swayed and staggered forward, in helpless violence, slaughtering and squandering on ever-increasing scales . . .' The Dardanelles was Churchill's attempt to find a way out of this escalating hysteria and calamity. Here, as in so many other places in his writing, Churchill emphasises his belief in the power of action by the individual. He repudiates utterly the notion that life, be it of the single human being or that of a whole society or indeed that of the whole species, is under the control of larger forces and structures. 'No one can tell that he may not some day set a stone rolling or take or neglect some ordinary step which in its consequences will alter the history of the world.'

The assertion of his own individual will meant, in practical terms, putting to decisively active use the great navy which he controlled and which, compared with the army in France had, in his view, too much of a passive and merely defensive role. His 'sincere wish' was 'to make the weight of the Navy tell as effectively as possible. This, I thought, was my duty.' This act of personal assertion immediately entailed a difficult psychological negotiation, some highly sophisticated in-fighting with two senior military men both much older than he. One was that continuing member of the *dramatis personae* of Churchill's eventful life, his adversary going back to the campaign in Egypt reported in *The River War*, Herbert Horatio Kitchener. Awarded an earldom and then brought back into the Cabinet as Minister of War in 1914, Kitchener and his moustachioed face would soon become one of the great poster images of the Great War accompanying the recruiting message: 'Your Country Needs You.' In 1915 Kitchener's 'prestige and authority were immense'. As Secretary for War he intimidated most of Asquith's cabinet and, says Churchill, with gentle but forceful irony, about the relationship between an imposing administrator and a bureaucracy, 'He had absorbed the whole War Office into his spacious personality.' The Field Marshal utterly refused to delegate any of his responsibilities, so 'it will be realised that the strain that descended upon the King's greatest subject was far more than mortal man could bear'.

The allied ships entered the Dardanelles. They progressed. The admiral in charge had a mental breakdown. The ships advanced again. The new admiral hesitated when he lost two ships in a minefield. But for Churchill back in London this was not the terrible turning point. This came when Kitchener in Cabinet lost faith and withdrew his support from Churchill; 'Lord Kitchener had changed his mind.' Churchill, whose perceptions of men and power and politics were usually intuitive, goes on to say in a very simple sentence, 'I felt that moment in an intense way a foreboding of disaster.' The feeling was abundantly justified by events. To Churchill a crucial reason for the defeat in the narrow straits of the Dardanelles was his personal loss of control over the mind of Kitchener. In London, rather than on the spot, the Turkish 'defences of the Dardanelles were to be reinforced by an insurmountable mental barrier'. Kitchener and Cabinet members who so readily deferred to him averted their eyes from what was slowly, agonisingly, turning into a disaster. They would not see. Churchill saw their wilful myopia as an image from a fairy story, or rather, a horror story. 'A wall of crystal, utterly immovable, began to tower up in the Narrows.'

In his seventh chapter Churchill turns to pondering the wisdom of his imposing the Dardanelles enterprise upon his number two at the

Admiralty, the 75-year-old Admiral Sir John Arbuthnot Fisher. Churchill's relationship with this temperamental, unpredictable figure from his father's generation continued to be complicated. At times Fisher was absolutely with Churchill in believing in the Dardanelles venture. He was for it 'whole hog' or, more usually, remembering his Latin, 'totus porcus'. But at other times the old man would have sudden doubts, deep suspicions and then submit his resignation. Once he hid himself away in London and refused to attend the Cabinet. With an unashamedly grand gesture the urbane Asquith commanded him to return in the King's name. Such behaviour clearly destabilised cabinet resolve and momentum. Fisher's final resignation effectively brought down the Liberal government. As he looks back, Churchill repeatedly asks himself if he made a human as well as a political mistake in 'the great and continuous pressure I put upon the old Admiral'. 'Was it wrong to put this pressure upon the First Sea Lord?' Churchill finally concludes: 'I cannot think so.' For, 'once the choice has been made, then the business must be carried through in loyal comradeship'. 'Searching my heart, I cannot regret the effort. It was good to go as far as we did.' In *The World Crisis* Churchill rarely blames individuals. He has a larger human and literary interest in the nature of the group will and in perseverance as a collective virtue. For the failure of the latter was the great failing at the Dardanelles. 'Not to persevere – that was the crime.'

For Churchill, that sudden, total, mysterious loss of confidence on the part of old men in the Cabinet confirmed and assisted and even exaggerated the uncertainty of the naval commanders in the Dardanelles straits. The setback caused by the minefields was less damaging than the disproportionate loss of confidence by Cabinet members in London. Churchill, looking back on this turning point in his aggressive middle age, would always maintain that the naval officers on the spot should not have been daunted by the mines. Had they and their political superiors at Westminster been more determined, they would have been successful. Subsequent evidence concerning the number of mines the Turks and Germans had been able to lay suggests that he was right. But the hesitation and the inaction were decisive. The naval attack finally got nowhere and had to be replaced by a ground attack which proved disastrous. Fisher resigned for the last time, the government fell and Churchill was dismissed from the control of the Royal Navy. For the rest of his life Churchill's mind dwelled on the Dardanelles as a grand visionary strategy virtually unlimited in promise and potential. But, 'From all this reward and opportunity Fisher, by his own impulsive, fatal act, and I, through causes which these pages expose, were for ever disinherited.'

The climax of the tragedy had come. What is left in this volume is the bitterness of failure. The chapter titles set the tone: 'The Darkening Scene'. 'The Ruin Of The Balkans', 'The Abandonment Of The Dardanelles'. For the General who, as Churchill saw it, had the ignominy of presiding over this last chapter Churchill reserves a lashing contempt intensified by the classical allusion. 'General Monro was an officer of swift decision. He came, he saw, he capitulated.' Such contempt pulses through the last chapters, though it is often contained within urbane, decorous antitheses which recall Dr Johnson. The moment of the failure of the Cabinet's group will is often returned to. 'From this moment the perplexities of the British Government came to an end. Henceforward they remained steadfast in pusillanimous resolve.'

And what was left after the failure of the great initiative at the Dardanelles? Just more and more of that foul butchery of a war on the Western Front which Churchill had struggled, obviously most disingenuously, to justify to Siegfried Sassoon. The war going on in France was an affront to that former cavalry officer of Victorian times who had been taught, amazing though this may be to readers of the late twentieth century, to think of war as an art form. *The World Crisis 1915* concludes with a sarcastic account of the return to exclusive concern with the war on the Western Front and of the horrors this entailed. Here is just one sarcastic sentence, racing along in its outrage about such warfare: 'Good, plain straightforward frontal attacks by valiant flesh and blood against wire and machine guns, "killing Germans" while Germans killed Allies twice as often, calling out the men of forty, of fifty, and even of fifty-five, and the youths of eighteen, sending the wounded soldiers back three or four times over into the shambles – such were the sole manifestations now reserved for the military art.'

IV

There was a three-year delay between the appearance of this second volume and that of its successor, *The World Crisis 1916–18*, which came out in 1927. The delay was caused by Churchill's eventual return to the House of Commons and by his utterly unexpected appointment to one of the highest positions in government. A defeated Liberal in 1922, Churchill soon started to make his way back to the Conservative party. The Liberals were demoralised and hopelessly divided into two factions, one led by the patrician Asquith and the other by the now discredited demagogue Lloyd George. Churchill was especially angered that the Liberals allowed and sustained the minority Labour government formed in January 1924. When that government fell, there was a General Election in the October of that year. Becoming slowly reconciled to the Conservative party which he had abandoned almost twenty years before, Churchill was elected member for Woodford in Essex, a constituency which in its various subsequent forms he was to represent for the remaining forty years of his political life. The pleasure of this return to the House after two years of homelessness in the political wilderness was feverishly intensified when the new Tory Prime Minister offered Churchill one of the two highest-ranking Cabinet positions. The Prime Minister was Stanley Baldwin, a wealthy Midlands industrialist, a quiet, modest, pipe-smoking Conservative whose style was that of the ordinary man rather than that of the Tory aristocrat. He decided to involve Churchill in his government rather than leave him to operate as a critic outside it. He invited him to become Chancellor of the Exchequer. At the interview with Baldwin in 10 Downing Street, Churchill, surprised and excited, wept with happiness. The Exchequer had been his father's highest political achievement. Winston had carefully packed away and preserved the court robes of that office which his father had worn almost forty years before. He hurried off from Downing Street to unwrap them.

Churchill's most remembered act during his years as Chancellor during the second half of the 1920s was his restoration in 1925, under pressure from international financiers, of the Gold Standard. This policy was, in the view of many, including Maynard Keynes, the author of *The Economic Consequences of Mr Churchill*, highly detrimental to the industrial wellbeing of the country. And indeed there soon followed a good deal of disruption, which climaxed in 1926 when the colliery owners demanded that their miners accept both pay cuts and longer hours. When the National Union of Mineworkers in May 1926 refused these demands, the mine-owners locked out the men. Appalled by this treatment of the miners, the other major national unions immediately went on strike in sympathy. Britain suddenly found itself brought to a halt by the effects of a General Strike. At this moment of national crisis Churchill found a new opportunity to use his abilities as a writer. With all the other Fleet Street newspapers closed down by the strike, Churchill founded and directed a government newspaper, the *British Gazette*. He also wrote aggressive leading articles for it, sometimes over the name of other politicians. Ever mindful of the Bolshevik revolution of less than ten years earlier and, as Chancellor, all too well aware of the shakiness of the capitalist system in Britain at the time, Churchill wrote stridently against those who would overthrow the state. The threat of revolution, responded the *British Worker*, the paper established by the Trade Union Congress to answer the Conservative government's paper, 'exists nowhere save in Mr Churchill's heated and disorderly imagination'.

The Cabinet had envisioned the *British Gazette* as essentially an information sheet, but Churchill ran it, very energetically, as a propaganda organ for the breaking of the strike. He also tried to take over the recently founded BBC radio, or 'wireless', but was prevented by Baldwin and other cabinet moderates. In little more than a week the General Strike ended in failure. But in that time Churchill had built the circulation of the *British Gazette* to well over two million. It was generally regarded as an impressive achievement. But the harshness of his editorials against the workers, protesting obvious oppression, troubled his government colleagues, would long be held against him and would significantly affect his political career in later years.

All through these times of high political drama Churchill worked steadily, with the dedication of the professional writer, at the continuation of his *World Crisis*. He now wrote in his study at his newly acquired country house, Chartwell Manor, near Westerham in Kent. On coming into a substantial and unexpected inheritance in 1921, Churchill had set about looking for a country property. When shown Chartwell, Churchill instantly fell in love with the place, its undulating green acres and its dramatic views down over the Weald of Kent and the North Downs. Clementine, more realistically, noted the poor layout of the house, its dry rot and its generally dilapidated state. She voiced her objections with characteristic force and believed that she had convinced Winston of the ridiculousness of even considering such a property. But in secret Churchill continued to negotiate with the estate agents, Knight, Frank and Rutley. He tried to force the price down and behaved with very bad grace when he failed to do this. But just a few months before his career as a Coalition minister ended in 1922, Churchill bought Chartwell for £5,000, without any consultation with Clementine whatsoever. Clementine was incensed when she was told. She hated Chartwell all the more and the house was to continue as another bitter cause of division in the marriage for a long time. The necessary refurbishment and extensions to the run-down house were to drain them of both the new inheritance and of the considerable sums of money earned by the successive volumes of *The World Crisis*.

But it was in his study at Chartwell that Churchill finished the next volume of this large undertaking, the first of many of his literary works to be completed there. This third volume, dealing with the years

1916–18, begins with an apology from the author, now Chancellor of the Exchequer, for the delay in continuing the story of the time after his great comedown in 1915. 'All arrangements had been made to publish this third volume of *The World Crisis* two years ago.' But: 'I was invited to take office in the present government.' And: 'The weight of my official duties forced me to put literary projects indefinitely aside.' Yet for all the pressures of government work upon him, Churchill here writes with a good deal of energy and vitality. A great stimulus to his literary imagination at this time was a growing and passionate interest in the England of the last decade of the seventeenth century and of the following twelve years which made up the reign of Queen Anne. This interest led Churchill a few years later to undertake a massive biography of the great figure of the England of that period, his ancestor John, Duke of Marlborough. In that work the great European crisis of Marlborough's time will be represented as an analogue of the great crisis of Churchill's time. But for the moment, in 1927, it is Marlborough's younger contemporary, the novelist and prose writer Daniel Defoe, who intrigues the author continuing with *The World Crisis* and helps his literary confidence. What interests Churchill are not Defoe's famous novels such as *Robinson Crusoe* and *Moll Flanders* but rather his *Memoirs of a Cavalier* of 1720, which tells the story of a young Shropshire gentleman in his many campaigns and exploits, first in the service of the Swedish king, Gustavus Adolphus, and then of his own sovereign, King Charles I, during the Civil War in England. What Churchill calls 'this delightful work' serves him as a reference point and a confirmation in handling the literary problem of writing simultaneously personal history and European history, that difficult amalgam which is the subject of *The World Crisis*. Defoe, remarks Churchill in the preface to the new volume, 'hangs the chronicle and discussion of great military and political events upon the thread of the personal experience of an individual'. Churchill was pleased to discover that he had hit upon the same method as a writer of Defoe's stature.

> I was immensely encouraged to find that I had been unconsciously following with halting steps the example of so great a master of narrative. In this present volume I try to present the reader at once with a comprehensive view of the mighty panorama and with a selection of its dominating features; but I also tell my own story and survey the scene from my own subordinate though responsible station.

The early chapters of Churchill's account of the last two or three years of the Great War tilt more towards the public world than the personal experience of the narrator. They are generally far less to do with the author himself than is the case with the preceding volume, *The World Crisis 1915*. The later book is based in considerable part on wide and extensive reading in other books on the subject. An area of reading which always compelled Churchill's interest was military history, a subject in which he was both a scholar and a connoisseur. One of the classic authors in this field is the French writer of the time of the Revolution, the Comte de Ségur, the great French prose stylist who wrote what Churchill calls a 'captivating account' of Napoleon's long march through Russia to Moscow. Churchill recalls this work as he comments upon and uses a book published by a British staff officer in 1922 entitled *Sir Douglas Haig's Command 1915–1918*. A French staff officer one hundred years before had sought to defend the Emperor against the criticisms of de Ségur; his book, says Churchill, had made Napoleon look worse than Ségur's comments had done. Similarly Haig's staff officer's attempt to defend his general clearly and comically defeats itself. It is part of the urbanity of Churchill's history-telling that he has such resources of contextualisation.

Haig's staff officer is an important source for Churchill; his book also amuses him. Churchill remarks, 'His work is aggressive to a degree that sometimes ceases to be good-natured. It is marred by small recriminations, by an air of soreness, by a series of literary sniffs and snorts which combine to produce an unpleasant impression on the mind of the general reader.' But, with all its bluntness and bad temper, the book is a valuable one. 'With all its faults, indeed to some extent because of them, *Sir Douglas Haig's Command* is a document of real value . . . There are none of those reticences and suave phrasings with which the successful actors on the world-stage are often contented when they condescend to tell their tale. Here we have the record of actual feelings unadorned.'

As the contrast made here suggests, Churchill is always aware of the gap between bland official language and the language that expresses felt realities. As he comes to write the painful chapter 'The Battle Of The Somme', he begins by remembering the poet Siegfried Sassoon, whose work had forced on him the tormenting irreconcilability of received principle and the actualities of experience in the terrible war. He places two lines from Sassoon at the head of his chapter as its epigraph.

> Pray God that you may never know
> The Hell where youth and laughter go.

As Churchill's prose conveys the larger movement of such terrible, inhuman battles (the Somme involving 'the greatest loss and slaughter sustained in a single day in the whole history of the British army'), it also pauses to linger on individuals, General Sir Henry Parkinson, for example, the commander of the British 4th Army on the Somme. Defoe's pendulum has tilted back and a particular person known to Churchill is before us in an economical prose vignette. Sir Henry is, like Ian Hamilton, the scholar-soldier, the well-read student of war as art and science, 'a tough cheery gentleman and sportsman' in whom can also be perceived, says Churchill, the intellectual dedication of his forebears, one of whom produced *A History of Assyria* and another a version of Herodotus.

In the final chapters American troops arrive in France to support the Allies (a development much dwelled upon by Churchill), the last terrible battles are fought, the Germans, somewhat surprisingly, exhaust themselves and collapse and the armistice is agreed. All the battles leading up to this finale have been described in a prose that has a strong, sound quality. Churchill's way of writing from this time on was often to dictate to secretaries. And the resonance and sometimes the rhetoric of the orator can be heard in this writing. The prose is very often the sounding language of the oral poet relating great battles. And yet it all ends in a movement to silence, as Defoe's personal point of view resumes. The armistice comes ever closer, the eleventh hour of the eleventh day of the eleventh month of 1918 approaches and the Minister of Munitions stands at his window in the Metropole Hotel overlooking Northumberland Avenue, waiting for nearby Big Ben to sound out the historic hour. The rich, resonant, sometimes oratorical prose of the multi-volumed *The World Crisis* concludes with a quiet and simple sentence fragment. 'And then suddenly the first stroke of the chime.'

V

This near two-thousand-page version of recent history was a success for Churchill's publishers and in 1929 he added a sequel volume, *The Aftermath*, which also did well. Two years after that Churchill produced one more related volume, *The Eastern Front*. But this work, published as the great economic depression of the thirties set in, aroused far less interest and with it *The World Crisis*, as a sequence, came to an end. *The Aftermath* is the more vivid and integrated coda. The story Churchill tells covers roughly the two years following that Armistice Night of hysterical jubilation in Trafalgar Square and Lloyd George's quiet but deeply contented dinner at 10 Downing Street which Churchill attended. They are two eventful years which, as a result of events in central Europe, Versailles, Greece and Ireland, created both the shape and the problems of Europe and the North Atlantic for the remainder of this century.

Several chapters are devoted to the development of the Russian Revolution, the leaders of which are presented in mythical terms as figures of absolute evil. Lenin, 'a plague bacillus', is associated with the Devil in Goethe's *Faust*. He is the unfathomably negative spirit that destroys and denies everything. In his fourth chapter, 'Russia Forlorn', in which Churchill describes the newly established Soviet government debating the claims of consolidating 'socialism in one country' as opposed to the call for the violent exporting of the revolution, Churchill writes ever more bitterly and fanatically. The comparison he now uses is the elemental battle between good and evil as it is described in Milton's *Paradise Lost*. Churchill recalls the devils' debate in the first book of the epic and quotes lines from it. Then, turning to the urgent discussion among Russian revolutionary leaders, he goes on, 'Some details of this new debate in Pandemonium have been preserved. Trotsky, in the name of Moloch, urged the renewal of war, and the majority of the secret Assembly seemed to share his passion. The calm sombre voice of Lenin rallied them to their duty in a Belial discourse of eighteen theses.' During the years Churchill describes, there were still British troops in Russia who had originally been sent there to assist the Czarist ally in various ways. Churchill writes of his desperate attempts to keep them there to assist the White Russians seeking to defeat the Red Revolution. His passion to sustain Western intervention in Russia is fuelled by that demonologising of the revolution which shows in the use of the analogy from Milton.

The treaty-making at Versailles and the historic, heavily consequential decisions which, with difficulty and with much unhappy compromise, were made there constitute no such high drama of good and evil with Lenin as 'Vengeance'. The Versailles conference is shown as more of a comedy or even a farce. In his half-dozen chapters on the various stages of the development of negotiations, Churchill focuses especially on the role of the salvationist American President, Woodrow Wilson, the high-minded idealist (at least in foreign affairs) dealing with the worldly, cynical, corrupt Europeans who had brought disaster upon themselves. Churchill summarises Wilson's difficulties in domestic and international politics in a generalisation owing something to Dr Johnson. 'It is difficult for a man to do great things if he tries to combine a lambent charity embracing the whole world with the sharper forms of populist party strife.' There was a tension between the Wilson of Versailles and the Wilson of Washington DC. As the President sailed for France, remarks Churchill (in a characteristic antithetical sentence), 'before him lay the naughty entanglements of Paris; and behind him the sullen veto of the Senate.'

Churchill mocks an American reporter at the conference who ignores such difficulties and who is shaken, astonished when 'the hearty whole-souled American delegation' is suddenly confronted with the labyrinthine secrecies of the Europeans. 'No such effect had been produced,' remarks Churchill, offering a simile, 'since Fatima opened the secret chamber of Bluebeard.' For him such a view is a simplistic Hollywood view of political complexities. It is just 'a film tableau'. And to poke fun at such showbiz simplifications Churchill, the Miltonic scourge of Lenin, impersonates the theatrical impresario, urgently ordering: 'Tableau! Curtain! Slow music! Sobs; and afterwards chocolates!'

Between the tonal extremes of demonic tragedy and sentimental light comedy there is the very human drama of postwar Ireland. In January 1919, just two months after the Armistice, 'the Sinn Fein Congress met in Dublin and read a Declaration of Independence'. Exactly a week later, 'a Republican Parliament met at the Dublin Mansion House and elected a Cabinet'. The following year the British government produced The Government of Ireland Bill, proposing Home Rule for the greater part of Ireland but maintaining the union of the six predominantly Protestant counties of Ulster with Great Britain. Churchill as Colonial Secretary was the principle figure in the organising of the passage through the House of Commons of this Bill which was as offensive to right-wing Conservatives in London as it was to many Republicans in Dublin. During the lengthy, intricate negotiations Churchill came greatly to admire two of the Irish spokesmen. Michael Collins, on whose head the British had once put a price and who was soon to be assassinated by more uncompromising members of Sinn Fein, greatly impressed Churchill just as he impressed Churchill's friend, the Ulster Catholic painter Sir John Lavery. Churchill, always interested by the role of individual human character in politics, spends several paragraphs pondering this forceful Irishman. Michael Collins, he concludes, 'had elemental qualities and mother wit'. Another member of the Irish delegation to Downing Street was Arthur Griffiths, the first president of the new Irish Parliament, the Dail. A prominent Sinn Fein leader and the founder and editor of the *United Irishman*, he was also the kind of man with whom Churchill could quickly and easily relate. 'Mr Griffiths was a writer who had studied deeply European history and the polity of States . . .' He was also, adds Churchill, that very rare phenomenon, 'a silent Irishman'.

Churchill more than any other Englishman presided over the ending of colonial Ireland. And despite the loss of Collins and Griffiths so soon after he had come to know them, Churchill had great hopes for the newly founded Free State in the new order of nations created by the aftermath of the Great War. This feeling, expressed in a long rhetorical paragraph, is part of a wider optimism that informs this coda to *The World Crisis*. *The Aftermath* was published in 1929 and at the end of the book Churchill feels able, looking back, to suggest, as he had not been able to do in 1922, that the world crisis was at an end. But without his knowing it, in that same year of 1929, the year of the Great Crash on Wall Street, there was to begin a new and protracted crisis both in Churchill's own life and in that of the western world generally.

Within weeks of the publication of *The Aftermath* in 1929, the Conservative government in which Churchill the writer continued as Chancellor of the Exchequer was defeated in a General Election. As the election results came in, the foulness of Churchill's language shocked even the more hardened party workers and professionals. A second Labour government, again relying on the support of the Liberals, took office. For roughly ten years, from 1929 to 1939, Churchill would be excluded from government office. Such isolation would create considerable frustration and bitterness in him. But the dialectic of the literary and the political in his life continued to operate. The decade of the thirties, which was a misery to him as a politician, was a period of intense and very successful activity for him as a writer. In fact, in no decade was Churchill the writer more creative than in the 1930s. In these ten years the prose artist was to undertake, and to realise, some major literary achievements in prose forms that he had never previously attempted.

CHAPTER SIX

The Autobiographer

In the first week of June 1929 Churchill and the other ministers in the defeated Conservative government travelled by train from London to Windsor to hand back their seals of office to King George V. Losing his position as Chancellor of the Exchequer, Churchill also lost his ministerial salary. And now began the chronic financial problems that were to continue to plague him throughout the coming decade, problems that were immediately intensified by his heavy losses in the Wall Street crash later in 1929. Churchill's first response to his sudden loss of ministerial income was to work harder at selling his literary work. Earlier that year he had decided that his next major project would be a biography of his great ancestor John Churchill, the first Duke of Marlborough. On the strength of the success of *The Aftermath*, he succeeded in obtaining excellent advances on this idea from Harrap in London and, again, from Scribner's in New York. And from the moment he left 11 Downing Street, he worked at selling the serialisation rights on the Marlborough to William Berry, now Lord Camrose, the enterprising Welsh journalist who had made his way from obscurity to become editor-in-chief of the *Daily Telegraph*. On the second day of August that year Churchill wrote to accept Camrose's offer of, for those times, the substantial amount of £5,000.

The very next day Churchill continued his urgent quest for money by setting off to North America to give a series of lectures and speeches and to develop contacts. He sailed from Southampton for Quebec City on the *Empress of Australia*; he was accompanied by his brother Jack, his son Randolph and Jack's son Johnny. The two middle-aged brothers and the two teenage cousins travelled across Canada in a special luxury coach with private bathrooms, an observation room and a parlour, put at the disposal of the visiting celebrity by the Canadian Pacific Railroad Company. Churchill addressed meetings in Montreal, Ottawa, Toronto, Regina, Calgary and Vancouver. All these occasions were great successes for the famous statesman. He wrote to Clementine, 'Never in my whole life have I been welcomed with so much genuine interest and admiration as throughout this vast country. All parties and classes have mingled in the welcome. The workmen in the streets, the girls who work the lifts, the ex-servicemen, the farmers, up to the highest functionaries have shown such unaffected pleasure to see me and shake hands that I am profoundly touched . . .'

In Vancouver the party turned south into the United States. Facing the America of Prohibition, eighteen-year-old Randolph in Vancouver filled up two hip flasks and a collection of medicine bottles with brandy and Scotch. The fathers and sons travelled down through Washington and Oregon into California. Here they stayed with the vastly wealthy William Randolph Hearst at his large, architectural concoction of a mansion at San Simeon. Like most visitors, Churchill and his companions could not help but be impressed by the press magnate's sumptuously, if vulgarly, furnished castle. Churchill was also intrigued by what he termed Hearst's 'two charming wives', the actual Mrs Hearst and the resident mistress, Marion Davies, a pretty, bubbly, gin-loving star of silent movies who had begun her career in show business as a dancer in the Ziegfeld Follies. To Clementine Winston marvelled that this large, weird ménage was presided over by a man who had 'the appearance of a Quaker elder – or perhaps better, Mormon elder'. Yet Churchill got on very well with Hearst. And this was to prove useful to the journalistic side of Churchill's now expanding career as a writer. During the next few years his articles would be frequently, and very remuneratively, syndicated in Hearst's many newspapers.

Churchill's party proceeded to Hollywood, where he was the guest of honour at a grand lunch given by the Metro Goldwyn Mayer studios. The visitors were also entertained at Marion Davies's glamorous house, where they swam in her heated marble pool. Afterwards there was a formal dinner which was attended by more than sixty distinguished guests. One of these was the great film comedian Charlie Chaplin, whose career had begun in the music halls of south London. The grandson of the Duke of Marlborough was especially keen to meet his now wealthy fellow-countryman who had grown up in the slums of Lambeth. For Churchill had a business proposition to put to him.

Throughout the thirties Churchill made efforts to pursue a career as a writer of film scripts. He now urged on Chaplin the idea of a film about that long-standing Churchillian interest, Napoleon Bonaparte. The film was to focus on the young Napoleon, with Chaplin playing the lead and directing and Churchill supplying the script. Randolph recalled that 'Papa and Charlie sat up till about 3' discussing the project. Winston, reporting to Clementine, said how much he had enjoyed the meeting with the actor despite Chaplin's left-wing political attitudes. 'We made gt friends with Charlie Chaplin. You cd not help liking him. The boys were fascinated by him. He is a marvellous comedian-bolshy in politics and delightful in conversation. He acted his new film for us in a wonderful way. It is to be his gt attempt to prove that the silent drama or pantomime is superior to the new talkies. Certainly if patter and wit still count for anything it ought to win an easy victory.' But Churchill's own subsequent writing for the cinema was based on the idea and the technology of the sound film. He was alert to the aesthetic problems inherent in the new medium as his subsequent letters to the British film producer, Alexander Korda, show.

After five more nights in Los Angeles, in a luxury suite in the Biltmore Hotel donated by a wealthy admirer, the Churchills travelled eastwards and homewards in another private railway coach supplied this time by Charles Schwab, the chairman of the Bethlehem Steel Corporation of Pennsylvania, who had been a passionate supporter of the Allied cause during the Great War. The party went to the Grand Canyon, to Chicago and thence to New York, where they were the guests of the wealthy financier Bernard Baruch at his home on Fifth Avenue. The evening on which Baruch gave a dinner for Churchill and more than forty prominent businessmen and bankers was also, by a terrible and memorable irony, the evening of the historic financial crash on Wall Street. Churchill remembered that the plutocrat who stood up to propose the visitors' health addressed the gathering as 'Friends and *former* millionaires'. The following morning Churchill, high up in an expensive apartment, was a witness to the kind of human consequences which the disaster brought about. He described the suicide with the laconic, faintly ironic calm of one who had seen first-hand the horrors of the Great War. 'Under my window a gentleman cast himself down fifteen storeys and was dashed to pieces, causing a wild commotion and the arrival of the fire brigade.'

On his return to England Churchill wrote a sequence of articles about his recent experiences in the United States, which Lord Camrose published in the *Daily Telegraph* in twelve weekly instalments. Churchill tried hard to get these articles published in book form under the title 'American Impressions'. But publishers consistently rejected his proposal. Another projected book, this one dealing with socialism and provisionally entitled 'The Great Failure', also, in this time of Ramsay MacDonald's second Labour government, failed to interest a publisher. But with his next literary venture, the volume of autobiography entitled *My Early Life,* published in October 1930 by Thornton Butterworth, Churchill was to have both a literary and financial success.

Churchill's autobiography deals, for the most part, with his first quarter century. It is about the prelude to his career as a politician. It begins with his earliest childhood memories and ends (except for a gallant allusion in the last sentence to his marriage in 1908) in his twenty-sixth year, in 1902. The significance of this year, as Churchill recalls it, is that it was the time that he first started to disagree with the policies of the Conservative party, the party to which his family had long belonged and in whose interest he had entered Parliament some two years before. The growing disagreement would, of course, finally lead to the first of the great decisions in Churchill's political career, his crossing the floor to join the Liberal party. But *My Early Life* does not quite take us up to this first major act of his adulthood. It confines itself to his childhood, youth and early manhood. Its subject is what is characteristically the subject of the German *Bildungsroman*. It is an account of a formation and, in the broadest sense of the word, an education into full adulthood.

The book is about youth and throughout is a celebration of youth. Churchill writes, 'the years 1895 to 1900 which are the staple of this story exceed in vividness, variety and exertion anything I have known – except of course the opening months of the Great War'. Writing and publishing this autobiography when he is in his mid-fifties, Churchill is continually aware of a generation of readers younger than he. The book is dedicated 'To A New Generation'. And he ends his fourth chapter with a strong exhortation to its members: 'Come on now all you young men, all over the world. You are needed more than ever now to fill the gap of a generation shorn by the War. You have not an hour to lose. You must take your places in life's fighting line. Twenty to twenty-five! These are the years! Don't be content with things as they are . . . Don't take no for an answer. Never submit to failure . . . You will make all kinds of mistakes; but as long as you are generous and true and also fierce, you cannot hurt the world or even seriously distress her. She was made to be wooed and won by youth.'

In these sentences Churchill speaks not only to his readers; he speaks also of himself. The principle emotion recalled in the book is youthful joy. Churchill evokes infectiously the joys of adventuring, of fighting, of danger and of seeing the landscapes of the Indian frontier, of Egypt and South Africa. He also remembers the joy of becoming a writer and a successful one. Here is his memory of receiving the reviews of *The Malakand Field Force*: 'When the first bundle reached me . . . I was filled with pride and pleasure at the compliments . . . Now here was the great world with its leading literary newspapers and vigilant erudite critics, writing whole columns of praise! In fact I should blush even to transcribe the glowing terms in which my "style" was commended . . . I felt a new way of making a living and of asserting myself, opening splendidly out before me.'

But if youthful happiness is a predominant theme in *My Early Life*, Churchill also recalls the darker and more painful parts of his growing up. For the autobiographer in late middle age certain miseries and humiliations are still keenly felt. He vividly evokes his unsuccessful attempts to pass the entrance examination to Sandhurst, his father's seeming indifference to him, his failure to advance very far at Harrow and his utterly frustrating block as far as learning Latin was concerned. Very evidently this last misery created a lasting inferiority complex. It shows in the repeated, almost compulsive, jests and ironies about those who have had university educations. This is but one of the many psychological difficulties and complexities which the book concedes and which contribute to its interest and value as a literary work. The basic structure of the autobiography may be a simple one, the progress from demoralisation and self-doubt to achievement and joy. But the prose in which this process is recorded also does justice to the mutation of a personality of great depth and intricacy.

The feature of Churchill's prose style which most conspicuously assists his purpose is the very marked changes in tone. Take, for instance, his propensity for sudden self-depreciation. A typical example of this is his description of being invited to dinner, when a very young subaltern, by the Governor of an Indian province, Lord Sandhurst. The description of the grand social occasion becomes suddenly a recognition and a quiet mockery of a youthful Churchillian bumptiousness.

> His Excellency, after the health of the Queen-Empress had been drunk and dinner was over, was good enough to ask my opinion about several matters, and considering the magnificent character of his hospitality, I thought it would be unbecoming in me not to reply fully. I have forgotten the particular points of British and Indian affairs upon which he sought my counsel; all I can remember is that

> I responded generously. There were indeed moments when he seemed willing to impart his own views; but I thought it would be ungracious to put him to so much trouble and he very readily subsided.

The gentle irony of this is a recurrent feature of the style of the book. But sometimes the self-criticism is more explicit. Churchill in this autobiography records many occasions of solidarity with other people, occasions of fellowship and shared good feeling. There is the experience of combat, of playing and winning in polo matches, of intense discussions with a group of Conservatives of his own generation when they all entered politics. But there is also the Churchill who knows himself to be resented and criticised by others, as must inevitably be the case with any such dynamic and assertive personality. If Churchill portrays himself as gregarious, he also portrays himself as the outsider. This sense of himself as someone apart and very much the object of criticism begins with the success of his first book. There is not quite so much irony in Churchill's recollection of this.

> I now perceived that there were many ill-informed and ill-disposed people who did not take a favourable view of my activities. On the contrary they began to develop an adverse and even a hostile attitude. They began to say things like this: 'Who the devil is this fellow? How has he managed to get to these different campaigns? Why should he write for the papers and serve as an officer at the same time? Why should a subaltern praise or criticise his senior officers?' . . . Others proceeded to be actually abusive, and the expressions 'Medal-hunter' and Self-advertiser were used from time to time . . .

But then the irony returns. 'It is melancholy to be forced to record these less amiable aspects of human nature, which by a most curious and indeed unaccountable coincidence have always seemed to present themselves in the wake of my innocent footsteps, and even sometimes across the path on which I wished to proceed.'

The sense of himself as someone apart, which is expressed here in a tone that is partly injured, partly mocking and partly self-regarding, reveals itself in other passages. Churchill sees himself as an outsider in more ways than one. He is, for instance, a historical and generational outsider. He is aware of a new generation knocking on the door and wishes it well and encourages it. But he knows himself to be apart, and very distantly apart from it. He comes from a different time and an altogether different social order. The contrasting of then and now is one of the most insistent themes in the autobiography.

He announces it right at the outset in his preface. He observes: 'I find I have drawn a picture of a vanished age.' 'I was a child of the Victorian era, when the structure of our country seemed firmly set, when its position in trade and on the seas was unrivalled, and when the realisation of the greatness of our Empire and of our duty to preserve it was growing stronger.' Then comes a second term in the dialectic that informs his story, the England of 1930. 'Very different is the aspect of these anxious and dubious times.' The writer from the bygone age feels it necessary to request indulgence from his audience. 'Full allowance for such changes should be made by friendly readers.'

'Those days', the days of Churchill's youth in the nineties, are recurrently evoked. Here are some characteristic sentences:

> I gave myself over to the amusements of the London season. In those days English Society still existed in its old form. It was a brilliant and powerful body, with standards of conduct and methods of enforcing them now altogether forgotten. In a very large degree everyone knew everyone else and who they were. The hundred great families who had governed England for so many generations and had seen her rise to the pinnacle of her glory, were interrelated to an enormous extent by marriage. Everywhere one met friends and kinsfolk. The leading figures of Society were in many cases the leading statesmen in Parliament, and also the leading sportsmen on the Turf. Lord Salisbury was accustomed scrupulously to avoid calling a Cabinet when there was racing at Newmarket, and the House of Commons made a practice of adjourning for the Derby. In those days the glittering parties at Landsdowne House, Devonshire House or Stafford House comprised all the elements which made a gay and splendid social circle in close relation to the business of Parliament, the hierarchies of the Army and Navy, and the policy of the State.

What ended this kind of civilisation and marked the divide between the two Englands and the two selves of which he writes was the Great War of 1914–1918. One aspect of this vast change to which Churchill often returns in his autobiography is the change in the nature of war itself. At times the prose style of *My Early Life* approaches poetry – and never more so than when Churchill evokes his experience, as a young cavalry officer in the 4th Hussars, of riding in squadron.

> There is a thrill and charm of its own in the glittering jingle of a cavalry squadron manoeuvring at the trot; and this deepens into joyous excitement when the same evolutions are performed at a gallop. The stir of the horses, the clank of their equipment, the thrill

> of motion, the tossing plumes, the sense of incorporation in a living machine, the suave dignity of the uniform – all combine to make cavalry drill a fine thing in itself.

Churchill then goes on to deplore the loss of this 'fine thing'.

> It is a shame that War should have flung all this aside in its greedy, base opportunist march, and should turn instead to chemists in spectacles, and chauffeurs pulling the levers of aeroplanes or machine guns. But at Aldershot in 1895 none of these horrors had broken upon mankind. The Dragon, the Lancer and above all, as we believed, the Hussar, still claimed their time-honoured place upon the battlefield. War, which used to be cruel and magnificent, has now become cruel and squalid. In fact it has been completely spoilt. It is all the fault of Democracy and Science. From the moment that either of these meddlers and muddlers was allowed to take part in actual fighting, the doom of War was sealed. Instead of a small number of well-trained professionals championing their country's cause with ancient weapons and a beautiful intricacy of archaic manoeuvre, sustained at every moment by the applause of their nation, we now have entire populations, including even women and children, pitted against one another in brutish mutual extermination.

Churchill the poet is there in the phrase 'a beautiful intricacy of archaic manoeuvre'. Just two nouns and two adjectives are put together to create a disproportionate density of meaning and feeling. It is a phrase that could easily have come from one of the greatest war poems of this century, David Jones's 'In Parenthesis'.

Churchill writes poetic prose quite unselfconsciously. This element in his style usually emerges when he writes about war. An excellent example is the first seven paragraphs of the fifteenth chapter of the autobiography, the chapter entitled 'The Sensations Of A Cavalry Charge'. It is a very lyrical and richly descriptive passage evoking the tension, suspense and excitement Churchill experienced in the last few hours before the Battle of Omdurman. In any competent anthology of writing about warfare in the western tradition since Homer's *Iliad* such a passage would without question command a place. Churchill, as the above quotations show, thought and felt atavistically about war. And such emotions charge his style when he writes about it. The result is that the notion of Churchill the soldier is inadequate to indicate the kind of human being who emerges from the account of the military career and exploits that is here presented. The unashamed atavism concerning war creates something more and other than the recollections of the military historian, it inspires the poetry of the warrior. This last word is one not often used today, but it is indispensable for a complete description of the kind of self (and not just in terms of military experience) the development of which this autobiography records.

The passages of heroic style in the book are impressive because this is not the only style. They figure among other styles which testify to a larger, wider awareness on the part of the author and increase the literary quality of the book. One such mode of writing that needs to be mentioned is the humour. There is quite a lot of it and it comes with a pleasing incidentalness. For instance, as he approaches the end of his book, Churchill tells us of his preparations as a young man to stand for the Conservatives at Oldham. At that time it was a two-seat constituency and Churchill had expected to have as his fellow Tory candidate a Mr Mawdsley, with whom he had unsuccessfully contested the seat at the previous election. But sadly he discovers, and makes a point of reporting, 'Mr Mawdsley was no more. He was a very heavy man. He had taken a bath in a china vessel which had broken under his weight, inflicting injuries to which he eventually succumbed.'

Such gentle humour is part of what contributes to our sense of the large humanity and humaneness of this book. It has also to be said that there are certain passages, certain tonalities that are less pleasing, less impressive. There is the occasional pomposity and the occasional reactionary irritability. In his dislike for the modern world, Churchill sometimes sounds like one who had some inkling that he would experience the now unfolding decade of the 1930s as a political outsider and outcast.

But despite the occasional wart this literary self-portrait is an impressive one. It is one of Churchill's best books and belongs with those other great autobiographies which are so important an element in the history of English prose, works such as the *Autobiography* of John Stuart Mill and that of John Ruskin in the nineteenth century, and in the twentieth that of Bertrand Russell and that of W.B. Yeats.

CHAPTER SEVEN

The Essayist

Six weeks after publication *My Early Life* had sold over 8,000 copies in Britain and 5,000 in the United States. The publishers, Thornton Butterworth, were greatly pleased. And in less than a year they were arranging with Churchill to bring out a selection of his articles that had appeared in newspapers and magazines during the last ten years or so. Churchill chose his most substantial, least ephemeral pieces and arranged them in such an order as to create an anthology with continuity and thematic and tonal unity. He gave the volume of essays the title *Thoughts and Adventures* and it appeared in 1931. It came out a couple of weeks later in the United States, under the title *Amid These Storms*. As Churchill worked at organising what proved to be a highly successful collection of his shorter prose pieces, his political and personal fortunes deteriorated greatly. Returning to Britain after his triumphant tour of the United States, where he had been greeted everywhere as a political superstar, he found himself, increasingly, to be a political outsider and more and more at odds with his fellow Conservative MPs who now constituted the Opposition to Ramsay MacDonald's second Labour government. The chief subject of disagreement between Churchill and them was his opposition to Baldwin's cooperative attitude to Labour's policy of granting a greater degree of political independence to India in its political and religious entirety. Churchill the Victorian strongly maintained his imperialist thinking throughout the thirties. When, in Delhi, the British Viceroy entered into conversations with Mahatma Gandhi, the Indian spiritual and political leader who had once been a London barrister, Churchill scorned such a meeting, declaring in a speech, 'It is alarming and also nauseating to me to see Mr Gandhi, a seditious Middle Temple lawyer, now posing as a fakir of a type well-known in the East, striding half-naked up the steps of the Vice-regal palace while he is still organising and conducting a defiant campaign of civil disobedience, to parley on equal terms with the representative of the King-Emperor.' Churchill's intransigence on this issue finally led to a crisis in his relations with the majority of the members of the parliamentary Conservative party and its leader, Stanley Baldwin, in January 1930. Churchill then decided that he could not continue to serve as a member of Baldwin's 'Business Committee', or what today would be called his 'Shadow Cabinet'. This resignation began Churchill's near ten-year exclusion from the policy-making centre, the power-centre of the Conservative party. When the Labour government fell as a result of the great financial crisis of 1931 and the Conservatives entered into a national government headed by MacDonald, Baldwin did not recommend Churchill as one of the Conservatives to be given ministerial office. As the thirties went on, Churchill's views about the rise of Nazism in Germany were another reason for his ever greater estrangement from the majority opinion in the Conservative party.

Some ten months after his resignation from Baldwin's 'Business Committee', Churchill, now no more than a backbencher, set off again for the United States, chiefly to repair his painful financial position which had grown ever more distressing as the after-effects of the 1929 stockmarket crash, in which he had lost so much, continued to erode what little he had left. On this trip to New York, on the German passenger ship *Europa*, he was accompanied by Clementine and their 25-year-old daughter Diana. One evening soon after their arrival, after the three had dined together at their Manhattan hotel, the Waldorf Astoria, Churchill set off in a taxi to begin discussing his money difficulties with the successful speculator Bernard Baruch at his home on Fifth Avenue. The inexperienced taxi driver could not find the address and spent more than an hour crawling up and down Fifth Avenue looking for it. Worried about the meeting and with his exasperation mounting, Churchill decided to get out and find his destination for himself. He scrambled out of the cab, began striding across the road and was instantly knocked down by an oncoming car travelling at thirty miles an hour or more.

Churchill was badly knocked about. The impact bloodied his thighs and his forehead and cracked two of his ribs. He lay in the roadway unable to get up. A later consequence was that he developed pleurisy and had to remain in bed in hospital for a week, and then for another two weeks at the Waldorf Astoria. It was the worst physical blow he had suffered in his life, far worse than anything he had experienced in all his years of soldiering. From New York Clementine wrote to Randolph concerning Winston's intense depression about the three 'very heavy blows' of the last two years: 'First the loss of all that money in the crash, then the loss of his political position in the Conservative Party and now this terrible physical injury.'

Clementine accompanied her badly shaken husband to Nassau in the Bahamas, where he spent more time recuperating. Then he returned to America and to his postponed lecture series, which proved to be an immense success. Very sympathetic and enthusiastic audiences turned out in great numbers to hear him. His recurrent theme was the menace of communism and the desperate importance of an alliance of the English-speaking peoples against it. In Washington DC he visited President Hoover and then went on to the House of Representatives, where proceedings were suspended so that Congressmen might greet the visiting celebrity. Before sailing from New York on board the liner *Majestic*, Churchill had lengthy conversations with his American publisher Charles Scribner about long-term literary projects. He also had extended discussions with the editorial staff of *Collier's Magazine*.

When the *Majestic* docked in Southampton, Churchill was welcomed by a group of British admirers and by the present which they had bought for him to help compensate for his recent sufferings. This was a brand-new motorcar, a Daimler, which gave him great pleasure. The gift had been organised by the thirty-year-old Brendan Bracken, who had recently been elected Conservative MP for North Paddington. A financier and financial journalist, Bracken was often rumoured, erroneously, to be Churchill's natural son. But unquestionably he was to be one of Churchill's staunchest supporters and most practical helpers in his many difficulties during the thirties. Despite Clementine's scepticism about this energetic young man with the flaming red hair, he became one of the most influential members of the Chartwell set during the 1930s and after.

Following the drama and the great wave of popular sympathy that marked his American tour, Churchill returned to Chartwell to grapple again with the problems he had left behind him, the chief one still being that of money. In his excellent bibliography of Churchill's writings, Frederick Woods notes that in the thirties Churchill even employed his literary skills writing notes to appear on the boxes of jigsaw puzzles depicting famous battles such as Jutland and Blenheim produced by Waddingtons of Leeds. And he was sufficiently hard up that he accepted an offer made by the proprietor of the *News of the*

World, Lord Riddell, to write a series of twelve articles for that newspaper entitled 'The World's Great Stories'. The articles were to be essentially plot summaries with comments. Churchill, who had been ill again, this time with paratyphoid fever, was so pressured by other journalistic and literary work, especially by the immense amount of research required by the Marlborough biography, that he persuaded Eddie Marsh to help him choose and summarise the stories for the *News of the World* articles. On discussing this project with this always ready and kindly collaborator, Churchill wrote that some of the famous stories he was inclined to choose for re-telling were: Alexander Dumas's *The Count of Monte Cristo*, Rider Haggard's *She, Ben Hur,* Anatole France's *Thaïs* and *Uncle Tom's Cabin.* 'I have always liked *A Tale of Two Cities,'* Churchill added, 'and *Faust* is a fine tale to tell.'

The ever reliable Edward Marsh also helped Churchill to put his volume of essays *Thoughts and Adventures* into its final form ready for his publisher and printer. In fact Churchill was sufficiently harassed by other commitments that it fell to Marsh to write the preface to the collection. When he saw this preface Churchill was greatly impressed and amused by his old friend's ability to imitate his style. Certainly the first readers would have been unlikely to suspect that, for instance, the prefatory comment on the two rather sombre essays on futurology, 'Shall We All Commit Suicide?' and 'Fifty Years Hence', was not by Churchill himself. The richly rhetorical, paragraph-long sentence has the characteristic Churchillian tread, the recourse to large abstract nouns, Destruction and Enslavement, and the sudden, in context, scintillating phrase 'a dilettante Cassandra'. This is the sentence which Churchill's ghost wrote:

> Many of these papers touch on the lighter side of grave affairs, but I should be sorry if on this account my two nightmares were taken merely as the amusing speculations of a dilettante Cassandra; for they are offered in deadly earnest as a warning of what may easily come to pass if Civilisation cannot take itself in hand and turn its back on those Cities of Destruction to which Science holds the keys.

Thus Edward Marsh as purveyor of pastiche Churchill. But in the last lines of the preface Marsh comes closer to giving himself away when, promising 'a happy ending' to a book which takes up 'the pleasures of life', he concludes with a quotation, from the French, from one of his favourite authors, La Fontaine.

> *Le monde est vieux, dit-on; je le crois; cependant*
> *Il le faut amuser comme un enfant.*

In *Thoughts and Adventures* Churchill does certainly amuse. Of all his many volumes this collection of essays is the most relaxed, the most entertaining. It contains a good deal of quiet, laid-back humour, often at the author's expense. 'The Battle of Sidney Street' remembers and accepts the sarcasm directed at him for his excess of zeal in dealing with the anarchist incident more than twenty years before in 1910. 'My Spy Story' centres upon a personal anecdote about the spy mania which seized Britain in 1914, in the early weeks of the Great War, in which Churchill's enthusiasm and his keen, patriotic suspiciousness led him into error. 'Plugstreet' (the British soldier's way of pronouncing Ploegstreet), the section of the British line in Flanders in which Churchill served in 1916, is another confessional essay in self-delusion and the powers of a hasty imagination. The essay is a vignette of Churchill's time at the front, illustrating an old man's saying, quoted in the first paragraph, that life 'had been full of troubles most of which had never happened'.

A more extended piece of humour and good humour on the subject of humour is the excellent essay 'Cartoons and Cartoonists'. It begins with an economical account of this near art form as Churchill had known and enjoyed it from boyhood. He remembers Mr Gladstone represented by Sir John Tenniel in *Punch* in the classical style, as Julius Caesar. Gladstone was represented as 'an august being crowned with myrtle, entitled to the greatest respect, a sort of glorified headmaster'. 'So that,' concluded the young Winston, 'was what Julius Caesar was like, a good, great, splendid man!' In adulthood he was shocked to find that the cartoon image of Caesar as a Gladstonian figure was false. 'It was quite a surprise to me in later years to learn that Julius Caesar was the caucus manager of a political party in Rome, that his private life was a scandal, printable only in a learned tongue . . .'

In the fashion of the essayist Churchill continues to treat very personally a subject which in other prose forms would be treated more systematically and dispassionately. He remembers how his father, Lord Randolph, when 'depicted in conflict with Mr Gladstone', the 'magnificent Gladstone, dressed like the disreputable Julius Caesar', was always represented by Victorian cartoonists 'as a midget, a midget with enormous moustaches and great fierce, bulbous eyes'. 'To this day I get letters from old people asking me how tall my father really was.' And Churchill himself writes, of course, as a famous man much caricatured. He singles out Low as 'the greatest of our modern cartoonists'. Low, declares Churchill, was an Australian radical whose gibes 'at the established order of things, and especially at the British Empire' were based on envy. 'To jeer at its fatted soul was the delight of the green-eyed young Antipodean radical.' Churchill recalls some of the mockery which Low directed at him personally, but as

MR. CHURCHILL AND FRIEND

WINSTON : "*We have both made history and we have both written it. Let us exchange headgear.*"

At the time of the publication of Churchill's The World Crisis *in April 1923,* Punch *places him beside another soldier-historian and comments on the size of Churchill's head.*

with many other cartoonists who set out to mock him, and especially his hats (always shown as several sizes too small), he concludes, with another large, tolerant phrase from the French, 'I owe him no grudge. *Tout comprendre c'est tout pardonner.*' In fact, cartoons and cartoonists are a healthy part of the political process. They are, says Churchill, in his final, very up-beat paragraph, part of the cleansing tide, 'a great tide of good nature and comprehension in civilised mankind which sweeps to and fro and washes all the pebbles against each other, cleans the beach of seaweed, strawberry baskets and lobster-pots. Hurrah for the tide!'

A similar joviality informs the essay 'Election Memories', in which Churchill in 1930, after some thirty years in parliamentary politics, relives his election joys and pains from a position of ironic, amused retrospection. He is very much the old hand. 'If you wish to know about elections I am the person to tell you. I have actually fought more parliamentary elections than any living member of the House of Commons.' And he knows only too well the whole process of getting, or failing to get, elected, from the moment of being adopted by the local party association to those final, anxious, electioneering meetings. 'Well do I know the loyal laughter of the faithful chairman or vice-chairman of the Association as he hears the same old joke trotted out for the thirty-third time. My dear friend, I do sympathise with you, my heart bleeds for you. Think of all the other meetings where I shall have to make this joke, and you will have to give your enthusiastic "Ha, ha, ha! Hear, hear! Bravo!" Never mind. It cannot be helped. It is the way the Constitution works.'

Churchill also remembers how, early on in his political career, the suffragettes began to attack and to disrupt his election meetings; 'it was most provoking to anyone who cared about the style and form of his speech to be assailed by the continual, calculated, shrill interruptions. Just as you were reaching the most moving part of your peroration or the most intricate point in your argument, when things were going well and the audience was gripped, a high-pitched voice would ring out, "What about the women?"' Defeated at North West Manchester, Churchill, the Liberal, successfully contested Dundee, but here too the women campaigners pursued him. Indeed here the aggravation was especially intense, for 'a peculiarly virulent Scotch virago armed with a large dinner-bell interrupted every meeting to which she could obtain access'.

But for all the recurrent lightheartedness of tone, these essays also take up some serious issues in experience. And, in so doing, their manner is very much in the essentially humanist tradition of this particular prose genre as it originated in the writings of Montaigne and continued, in English, over the centuries in the practice of Bacon and Addison and Steele and Hazlitt down to the work, to take one instance, of Churchill's young thirties contemporary, George Orwell. Churchill's essays continue a chief convention of the form in being very much 'attempts', ventures at a subject that are in no way doctrinaire, didactic or closed-minded. One question about experience which Churchill repeatedly attempts in *Thoughts and Adventures* has to do with the relationship between destiny, chance and the will of the individual. One view of this matter is expressed in 'With The Grenadiers', another very vivid, personal account of his time in the trenches of the Western Front after his departure from government in the aftermath of the Dardanelles fiasco in late 1915. The essay concludes by relating an episode which might well have ended in Churchill being killed, 'but for chance'. From this experience he deduces the notion 'that everything depends upon chance'; at the same time he cannot believe that chance 'arises from the blind interplay of events'. Chance itself, he essays, is a device, a function of some larger force. 'Chance, Fortune, Luck, Destiny, Fate, Providence seem to me only different ways of expressing the same thing, to wit, that a man's own contribution to his life story is continually dominated by an external superior power.' And attempts to avoid the effects of this power are, he ventures further, perhaps ways of making sure of encountering them. Once again the seventeenth-century poet and moralist La Fontaine appears in this volume as Churchill commends to his reader the lines:

On rencontre sa destinée
Souvent par des chemins qu'on prend pour l'éviter.

But it is part of the nature of the true essayist not to rest content with just one answer to a question about experience but rather to try out, and to explore, others. In another essay, 'Mass Effects In Modern Life', he begins by again accepting 'the decisive part which accident and chance play at every moment', but then is more sceptical about the idea of 'an external superior power' such as he had written about in 'With The Grenadiers'. 'Mass Effects In Modern Life' in fact goes on to take the view of 'the past history of the world as the tale of exceptional human beings, whose thoughts, actions, qualities, virtues, triumphs, weaknesses and crimes have dominated the fortunes of the race'. The essay then becomes a regretful pondering of what the essayist sees as the loss of conspicuous, active individualism in the ever more technological twentieth century. He recalls the Liberal statesman and writer, once Churchill's senior Cabinet colleague, John Morley, the biographer of Gladstone and also of Voltaire, Rousseau and Burke, who 'towards the close of his life delivered an oration in which he drew attention to the decline in the personal eminence of the leaders in almost all the important areas of thought and art. He contrasted the heads of the great professions in the early twentieth century with those who had shone in the mid-Victorian era. He spoke of 'the vacant Thrones in Philosophy, History, Economics, Oratory, Statecraft, Poetry, Literature, Painting, Sculpture and Music . . .' Churchill the late-Victorian shares the sense of loss felt by this mid-Victorian in facing a prospect of vacant Thrones, a prospect in which human beings lose the power for eminence and for agency. For Churchill the prospect is especially vivid in twentieth-century warfare. The essay becomes a celebration of, and a lament for, the passing of the power of human agency in this particular sphere. Remembering the horrors of the Great War, he contrasts highly personalised generalship in earlier centuries with that more anonymous form created by the technological warfare of the present day.

> No longer will Hannibal and Caesar, Turenne and Marlborough, Frederick and Napoleon, sit their horses on the battlefield and by their words and gestures direct and dominate between dawn and dusk the course of a supreme event. No longer will their fame and presence cheer their struggling soldiers. No longer will they share their perils, rekindle their spirits and restore the day . . . Instead our Generals are to be found on the day of battle at their desks in their offices fifty or sixty miles from the front, anxiously listening to the tinkle of the telephone for all the world as if they were speculators with large holdings when the market is disturbed.

Churchill then pursues this analogy in an extended metaphor. Soldiering and the vagaries of the stockmarket had both been important experiences in his life. He is pained to witness the heroic personal initiatives which he associates with the former replaced by the impersonal technical skills needed to deal with the latter. His metaphor is a long and virtuoso one; it is also , with its final equation of stockmarket and stockyard, a very powerful one. The metaphor starts quietly but, with that last word 'stockyard', ends with a disgust and a bitterness born of Churchill's memories of the unprecedented horrors of the warfare on the Western Front.

> Calm sits the General; he is a high-souled spectator. He is experienced in finance. He has survived many market crashes. His reserves are ample and mobile. He watches for the proper moment, or proper day – for battles now last for months – and then launches them to the attack. He is a fine tactician, and knows the wiles of bull

> and bear, of attack and defence to a nicety. His commands are uttered with decision. Sell fifty thousand of this. Buy at the market a hundred thousand of that. Ah! No, we are on the wrong track. It is not shares he is dealing in. It is the lives of scores of thousands of men. To look at him at work in his office you would never have believed that he was fighting a battle in command of armies ten times as large and a hundred times as powerful as any that Napoleon led. We must praise him if he does his work well, if he sends the right messages, and spends the right troops, and buys the best positions. But it is hard to feel that he is the hero. No; he is not the hero. He is the manager of a stockmarket, or a stockyard.

The most horrifying example of this kind of generalship is that of Ludendorff, who was in charge of Germany's last desperate offensive in the spring and summer of 1918. This is the subject of the essay 'Ludendorff's "All – Or Nothing"'. It is an occasion to which Churchill will return in his later writings. This was the 'most unhuman (in the sense of being wholly impersonal) of all the battles in the annals of war'. It was a terrible mid-life shock to Churchill, the former cavalry officer who had been brought up on nineteenth-century ideas of warfare. It was the final degradation of what as a Victorian he had been taught to honour as 'the art of war'; '. . . at this melancholy and degraded epoch it represents little but the massing of gigantic agencies for the slaughter of men by machinery'. And again the simile of disgust: 'It is reduced to a business like the stockyards of Chicago.'

The essay that follows immediately after this one is so placed as to form a contrast and a further comment. It is entitled 'A Day With Clemenceau' and is a vivid evocation of the Prime Minister of France during the last climactic months of the Great War and one of the great figures at Versailles during the subsequent time of treaty-making. Churchill is clearly in awe of 'The Tiger', the veteran political infighter, thirty years older than himself, who had been mayor of Montmartre way back at the time of the German siege of Paris in 1870 and who, later, had been a prominent defender of Dreyfus against his anti-semitic enemies. Clemenceau, who, like Churchill, was also a writer, was notorious for his devastating treatment of his opponents. But Churchill the essayist, as usual resorting to particulars, remembers him, and presents him, as charming and even amusing on the occasion in 1918 when Churchill was sent by Lloyd George to review the Allied military situation in France. On his arrival in France the British Minister of Munitions received the welcoming message, 'Not only shall Winston Churchill see everything, but I myself will take him tomorrow to the battle . . .' When they conferred, Churchill was struck by Clemenceau's 'extraordinary methods of exposition: his animation, his gestures, his habit of using his whole body to emphasise and illustrate . . . his vivid descriptions, his violence and vehemence of utterance'.

Slow to eat the food that was offered on their visit to British headquarters, Clemenceau waited 'until his contribution of chicken and sandwiches of the most superior type had been produced from the last of his cars'. This is the kind of illuminating detail that is characteristic of Churchill as essayist. But the central emphasis in this attempt at a brief sketch of Clemenceau is the man's sheer bravery. He was always ready, even eager, to go into the front line and experience the reality of it. Ludendorff is for Churchill a tactic, an abstraction, but Clemenceau is a very particular man, and one of great presence. 'The Tiger' is the very antithesis of the stockmarket/stockyard leader who manages a war from some fifty miles away. His zeal to get into the action is such that when they visit the British lines, Churchill, now his host, becomes alarmed. 'I thought on the whole we had gone quite far enough. If anything happened to this thin line . . . It would be very awkward if a sudden retirement of the line made it necessary for the Prime Minister of France to retreat directly across the fields and ford the river.' The feeling informing this essay is contained in the brief paragraph of verbal salute to Clemenceau, formally recorded, just three paragraphs from the end. Churchill warns Clemenceau about risking his life and receives a reply which he feels is important, revealing, to record: 'When I had a chance I said to him apart: "This sort of excursion is all right for a single day; but you ought not to go under fire too often." He replied – and I record it – "*C'est mon grand plaisir.*"'

A glimpse, a fleeting sense of a human personality is offered in many of the other essays. In 'Personal Contacts' Churchill ponders a succession of individuals whose effect upon him may be seen as part of his fate. Appearing to refute the determinism of 'With The Grenadiers', he maintains that 'the glory of human nature lies in our seeming capacity to exercise conscious control of our destiny'. But at the same time he also acknowledges those who have helped make him what he is, those currents that have played 'their part in the movements of the vessel that bears us onwards'. First among these is that deeply revered figure who recurs so often in Winston Churchill's writings, his father, Lord Randolph Churchill. Next he remembers his mother's lover, the prominent New York politician Bourke Cockran. This colourful personality is especially interesting to Churchill in this essay as one who changed his political allegiance, abandoning the Democratic party to join the Republicans. Another essay, 'Consistency In Politics', also takes up this matter which had been both painful and influential in Churchill's life. Here he argues that what may look like betrayal can in fact be consistency. A principle piece of evidence which he produces to justify this view is the career of one of his greatest literary admirations, Edmund Burke. 'No greater example in this field can be found than Burke.' 'His *Thoughts in the Present Discontents*, his writings and speeches on the conciliation of America, form the main and lasting armoury of Liberal opinion throughout the English-speaking world.' On the other hand, Burke's writings of the time of the French Revolution, his '*Letters on a Regicide Peace* and *Reflections on the French Revolution* [sic] will continue to furnish Conservatives for all time with the most formidable array of opposing weapons. On the one hand he is revealed as a foremost apostle of Liberty, on the other as the redoubtable champion of Authority.' But, insists Churchill, it would be vulgar to suggest that there was any duplicity in the career of this so distinguished man; '. . . a charge of political inconsistency applied to this great life appears a mean and petty thing'. 'No one can read the Burke of Liberty and the Burke of Authority without feeling that here was the same man pursuing the same ends, seeking the same ideals of society and government, and defending them from assaults, now from one extreme, now from the other.'

Always in these essays Churchill insists upon an individual human being, such as Edmund Burke, as being more important than abstractions and the depersonalisations of stockmarket generalship. And though a man of a much earlier generation than that of the revolutionary literary modernists of the 1910s, T.S. Eliot, Ezra Pound and D.H. Lawrence, Churchill shares their primary insistence on the specific, and on a particular human being. 'Personal Contacts' is in part an essay on the specific force, the emanations, of such individual human beings, of, for instance, the political friend of his youth, the Hughlian, Lord Hugh Cecil, 'a real Tory, a being out of the seventeenth century, but equipped with every modern convenience'. And then at the very end of the essay comes that last great Liberal Prime Minister, Lloyd George. Writing in the thirties, when he was again bitterly estranged from the Conservative party which he had rejoined in the early twenties, Churchill recalls the first time he had left the Conservatives and brought upon himself charges of disloyalty and treachery. 'When I crossed the floor of the House and left the Conservative Party in 1904, it was by his side that I took my seat.' Churchill spends two pages in essaying the reasons for the extraordinary powers of Lloyd George, of this man who so 'greatly influenced me'. 'Why was it that the Welsh wizard could, at his best, almost talk a bird out of a tree?' Churchill's list of attempted answers runs on and on: 'An intense comprehension of the more amiable weaknesses of human nature: a sure gift of getting on the right side of a man from the beginning of a talk: a complete avoidance of anything in the nature of chop-logic reasoning: deft touch in dealing with realities . . .' Looking back on the dumping of the Lloyd George coalition government in 1922 by the Conservatives, Churchill, the again estranged Conservative of the thirties, turns the tables on those who criticise him for political inconsistency and writes with mocking irony about the Baldwin Conservatives who are prepared to be part of a national government that includes the likes of the socialist Ramsay MacDonald. 'They have for the present happily settled down, for a while, under a Socialist, a wartime Pacifist, an anti-Imperialist, and a supporter of the General Strike. But it is understood that he will not interfere with Tory policy. L.G. is taboo.'

Thoughts And Adventures attempts to understand many diverse characters, sensibilities and personalities. But the personality that dominates this sequence of personal pieces is that of Churchill himself. In this collection more than in any other of his books we are aware of him and of the variety and complexity of his mind and feelings. The very last essay, for instance – a substantial piece entitled 'Painting As A Pastime' – is not just the story of how he came to take up painting but also of the swift development of a sophisticated eye both for the achievement of certain old masters and of the radically innovative art of the early years of this century. It is not customary to dwell on Churchill's artistic sensibility but here it is, fully described in both its origins and evolution. The essay is playfully evangelical in tone, full of imperative verbs urging the reader to have a go at painting and so share the author's intense pleasure in the activity. He recalls how he first attempted to paint at the time of his traumatic departure from the Admiralty in 1915; '. . . then it was that the Muse of Painting came to my rescue'. On that actual day the Muse took the form of Lady Lavery, the American wife of the Ulster painter, Churchill's friend, Sir John Lavery. As Churchill hesitated in front of that very first canvas Lady Lavery, herself a highly accomplished artist, drove up in her motorcar and exclaimed: 'But what are you hesitating about? Let me have a brush, the big one.' Churchill looked on as she took over. 'Splash into the turpentine, wallop into the blue and white, frantic flourish on the palette, clean no longer, and then several large, fierce strokes and slashes of blue on the absolutely cowering canvas. Anyone could see that it could not hit back. No evil fate avenged the jaunty violence.'

The jokiness of this last Latinate sentence and the hint of mock epic are characteristic of this fine essay throughout. It is never solemn, even though it is about an occurrence that was of serious importance in Churchill's inner life. For attempting to paint led him to see the world afresh and, quite simply, to see new beauty in it. 'I found myself instinctively, as I walked, noting the tint and character of a leaf, the dreamy purple shades of mountains, the exquisite lacery of winter branches, the dim pale silhouettes of far horizons. And I had lived for over forty years without ever noticing any of them . . .' 'I think this heightened sense of observation of Nature is one of the chief delights that have come to me through trying to paint.' Practising painting also led Churchill to a new appreciation of the great painters of the past, especially Turner. He read Ruskin on Turner and endorsed Ruskin's estimate of him with a similar magisterial confidence. 'When we look at the largest Turners, canvases yards wide and tall, and observe that they are all done in one piece and represent one single second of time, and that every innumerable detail, however small, however distant, however subordinate, is set forth naturally and in its true proportion and relation, without effort, without failure, we must feel in the presence of an intellectual manifestation, the equal in quality and intensity of the finest achievements of warlike action, of forensic argument, or of scientific or philosophical adjudication.'

For all the admiring weightiness of these last few phrases serving to measure Turner's achievement, Churchill's writing about art in this essay is invariably simple and clear. It has none of the jargon to which art criticism is prone. But the unassumingness, the down-to-earth quality of his account of art make it that much more compelling for the reader. Not that Churchill's taste and understanding were unsophisticated. The essay was first written in 1921 and in it Churchill shows and explains his enthusiasm for painters such as Cézanne, Manet, Monet and Matisse, who, little more than a decade before, when represented in Roger Fry's pioneering exhibition 'Manet and the Post-Impressionists' at the Grafton Gallery, had scandalised and outraged many visitors to the show. Churchill, on the other hand, was greatly affected in his seeing and his thinking by the works of Cézanne; 'it was of great interest to me to come suddenly in contact with this entirely different way of looking at things'. 'Difficult? Fascinating!' Churchill's excitement and pleasure in the impressionists and post-impressionists run on as he compares their achievement with that of the English romantic poets.

> But surely we owe a debt to those who have so wonderfully vivified, brightened, and illuminated modern landscape painting. Have not Manet and Monet, Cézanne and Matisse, rendered to painting something of the same service which Keats and Shelley gave to

poetry after the solemn and ceremonious literary perfections of the eighteenth century? They have brought back to the pictorial art a new draught of *joie de vivre;* and the beauty of their work is instinct with gaiety, and floats in sparkling air.

'Painting as A Pastime' is a fitting conclusion to this patterned collection of essays. Gaiety, humour, *joie de vivre* such as are here emphasised make for the dominant mood of this entertaining book. It is an important essay in that it displays very clearly the utterly unpretentious, yet vital, aesthetic element of Churchill's mind. A great deal has been written of his powers as a politician, statesman, soldier and strategist. But we see from this essay that there was far more to his wide-ranging intelligence than such categories suggest. For nearly fifty years he practised the art of painting not just as a hobbyist but as someone who took both theory and practice very seriously. When in 1948 the acclaimed world statesman and future Nobel Prize winner for literature finally visited Aix-en-Provence and was able to visit the Cézanne country and to paint there, he disconcerted and dismayed his companions at dinner one night by interrupting the table talk to say 'rather gravely':

'I have had a wonderful life, full of many achievements. Every ambition I've ever had has been fulfilled – save one.'

'Oh, dear me, what is that?' said Mrs Churchill.

'I am not a great painter,' he said, looking slowly around the table.

For a few seconds the embarrassment was so complete that no one could bring himself to say anything.

To ignore or underestimate the artistic side of Winston Churchill is to obscure the full nature of his genius. He had serious ambitions with the medium of paint, as with the medium of words. Throughout the second half of his long life he always had with him in his time-off his easel and palette and brushes. And, of course, he always had in mind various, and usually very ambitious, literary projects. In politics the thirties were for Churchill a disappointing and frustrating time. But another part of his biography during these years is the story of a slow but sure progress to a most singular literary achievement. After some ten years of hard work and unremitting literary dedication, the accomplished essayist of *Thoughts And Adventures* also showed himself the master of another and larger prose form. For, just as the thirties drew to a close and just a few months before a vindicated Churchill received the historic call back to government, he put the finishing touches to a work of literature which, in its time and for its length, scale and vision was immense and extraordinary. It was his biography of his great ancestor, John Churchill, the first Duke of Marlborough.

CHAPTER EIGHT

The Grand Biography

During the thirties, when he was so often tormented by chronic financial difficulties, Churchill tried to develop many literary ideas which, finally, he was unable to bring to a successful conclusion. He continued, for instance, to be greatly interested in the possibility of writing a life of Napoleon. This project came very much to life when, in the summer of 1934, Churchill and his son went to stay with an old friend, the elderly Maxine Elliot, a wealthy American and former actress who had a villa, the Chateau de l'Horizon, on the French Riviera. From there, at the end of his holiday, Churchill planned to follow the road to Grenoble which Napoleon had taken after his escape from Elba. It excited him to be on Napoleon's historic route and he wrote home to Clementine: 'I really must try to write a Napoleon before I die. But the work piles up ahead and I wonder whether I shall have the time and strength.'

One piece of work taking up Churchill's time at this period was a film script. In September of this year there was confirmed a major opportunity for Churchill to further his ambitions as a screen-writer. Alexander Korda, the Hungarian-born film producer who had been based in Britain since the early thirties, wished to make a film commemorating the twenty-fifth anniversary of the accession of King George V, which would occur in the following year of 1935. Korda, whose many film credits were to include *The Third Man* in 1949 and *Richard III* with Laurence Olivier in 1955, offered Churchill the then very considerable sum of £10,000 for a completed script on the story of the King and his reign. Entrusting to Keith Feiling of Christchurch, Oxford, the work on another book for which he had recently contracted and received a substantial advance, *The History of the English-Speaking Peoples,* Churchill left England and devoted himself to writing his film script. He again allowed himself to become the guest of one of his wealthy friends who was able to entertain him in the part of the world in which he most enjoyed holidaying, the Mediterranean. On this occasion he and Clementine were received on board the yacht *Rosaura* owned by Lord Moyne, a member of the Guinness family, who had been one of Churchill's junior ministers when he was Chancellor of the Exchequer. During the last autumn of that year which saw the end of Hitler's first year in power and the Reichstag fire, the Churchills sailed leisurely from Marseilles to Athens and then to Beirut and then from Alexandria to Naples. During the voyage Churchill worked hard on the script, all the time writing letters to Korda explaining the kind of film aesthetics on which his scripting was based. In 1934 what Churchill called 'the talkie aspect' of films was still quite novel and he was very concerned to exploit it. He was especially anxious about the background music, wanting it at times to be dominant and at others 'barely perceptible'. And Churchill, who always in his writing was quick to refer to the classics, urged that he himself should be heard on the soundtrack and should 'speak some passages myself, like a Greek chorus, and thus put points that can be put in no other way'.

Churchill was a sincere admirer of the King and his film script was to be a story on a heroic scale. It was to dwell on the King's courage, in the first difficult year of his reign, in helping pass the Parliament Bill by promising to create a majority of Liberal peers to ensure its passage through the House of Lords. The film was also to stress the King's role in the Great War and in its politically and constitutionally difficult aftermath. Unfortunately the Korda/Churchill film was not made because of new legislation concerning film distribution which would have ruined the proposed timetable and budget. The producer and the same writer went on to consider developing a script on the history of powered flight and the birth of the RAF, to be entitled 'The Conquest of the Air'. In that same year Churchill was approached by John Corfield, the managing director of British National Films, and invited to write an original movie script about the life of Cecil Rhodes. But Churchill the screen-writer was contractually tied up with Korda's company and, though extremely interested in the proposal, had to turn it down. Always excited by the rapidly developing new technology of this century, Churchill as a writer was greatly taken with the possibilities of film. And it was a great disappointment to him, personal as well as financial, when it became impossible to proceed with the script about George V.

The year following the King's Silver Jubilee was also the year of the King's death and the accession and, within months, the abdication of his son Edward VIII. Churchill had deep sympathy for the young king in the constitutional difficulties brought on by his love for the American divorcee Wallis Simpson, and by his determination to marry her. When Stanley Baldwin and his Cabinet decided that the King's intentions necessitated his abdication, Churchill, yet again a Conservative outsider, was a passionate, if politically clumsy, supporter of the King. In his memoirs the King, later the Duke of Windsor, remembered how touched he had been when, after a lunch at the end of the abdication crisis, he had watched his confidant Churchill leave and had heard him reciting quietly but emotionally to himself Andrew Marvell's lines about Charles I:

> *He* nothing common did, or mean,
> Upon that memorable scene . . .

Some have seen Churchill's idealising of the King and his romantic view of his love affairs as sentimental. Certainly it can be seen as a coherent part of Churchill's larger imaginative life during these years. For Churchill too was a man politically rejected. And as a writer he happened to be immersed in researching the life of another great figure who had known spectacular, almost melodramatic rejection and downfall, again in great part due to his love for a woman. This was his great ancestor John Churchill, the first Duke of Marlborough. While in the world of practical politics at Westminster, Churchill battled unavailingly against the appeasement of Hitler and the repudiation of the King; in his imaginative world, in his study at Chartwell, he studied and pondered and analysed and relived and wrote down the life of one of the greatest battlers of the eighteenth century. During the thirties Churchill the writer, like Churchill the now back-bench politician, was intensely preoccupied with the drama of pre-eminence and downfall, acclaim and then vilification, glory and humiliation.

His life of Marlborough proved to be a massive four-volume work. Churchill devoted close to ten years of his life to it and, aside from the footnotes, bibliographies, appendices and numerous maps and illustrations, the work runs to well over 2,300 pages. It is a lively, long read, reminiscent in scale, as often in style, of some of the great prose works of the Victorian period such as those by Carlyle and Ruskin. But for all its great length, the biography maintains throughout a quick pace and a dynamic narrative line. Right up to the end there is suspense in the story as the reader prepares for the hero's downfall and terrible degradation which, even as he writes of John Churchill's times of triumph, Winston Churchill continually reminds us, are still to come. At the very end the author achieves a powerful emotional effect as the reader ends his long relationship with this long book. On the last page of the text, which is an assessment of his hero's life achievement, Churchill directs us to the facing page, on which is the portrait of the hero as a very young officer. This device and the attractive youthful image remind us forcibly how far we have come in time from John Churchill's obscure boyhood in a poverty-stricken cavalier's home during the last ten years of Cromwell's rule to the time, just before his shocking comedown and humiliation at the end of the reign of Queen Anne, when he was the most powerful military and political figure not just in Britain but throughout Europe.

During the thirties, as he worked at this long and involved story in his study at Chartwell, Churchill had above his desk there a large map of Europe. The ten often brilliantly successful military campaigns which created his ancestor's great fame were all conducted on the continent, chiefly in Flanders and the Low Countries, but also, in one case, as far east as Blenheim in Bavaria. But the European frame of reference in Winston Churchill's book is thematic as well as narrative. A principle contention of the biography is that the hero, so very English as he is shown to be, achieved greatness as someone who altered the course of European history. Marlborough's story, declares Churchill in the preface to the second volume, 'spreads beyond our own annals and enters, often decisively, during the ten tremendous years into the strange, gigantic story of Europe'. 'It is not till we reach Napoleon, the Emperor-statesman-captain that we see this threefold combination of functions – military, political and diplomatic – which was Marlborough's sphere, applied again upon a continental scale.' It was, Churchill continues elsewhere, the historic distinction of Marlborough, 'whose outlook was European', to have presided over 'an august league of nations which . . . successfully defended the liberties of Europe against the intolerance of totalitarian monarchy'.

The totalitarian monarch who menaced the league of nations was Louis XIV, who ruled over a Catholic France which in the first years of the eighteenth century had the economic, financial and military power to threaten the independence of its smaller neighbours such as the Protestant nations England and Holland, an increasingly degenerate Spain and the ramshackle and ineffectual Holy Roman Empire. For Winston Churchill telling the story of how Marlborough galvanised these very different countries into an effective alliance against French imperialism, the King of France is very much the villain of the tale. 'During the whole of his life Louis XIV was the curse and pest of

Europe. No worse enemy of human freedom has ever appeared in the trappings of polite civilisation . . . The veneer of culture and good manners, of brilliant ceremonies and elaborate etiquette only adds a heightening effect to the villainy of his life's story.' 'Better the barbarian conquerors,' exclaims Churchill, ever more enraged, 'than this expansionist, imperialist bully at Versailles', 'this high-heeled, beperiwigged dandy, strutting amid the bows and scrapes of mistresses and confessors to the torment of his age'. 'Petty and mediocre in all except his lusts and power the Sun King disturbed and harried mankind during more than fifty years of arrogant pomp.' With these and other sentences of denunciation from the first volume in mind, the reader is conditioned for the distaste, mockery and sarcasm which attach to the phrase 'the Great King' as this continues to reappear right through to the end of the work. *Marlborough: His Life And Times* is very much a story of good and evil, a morality tale in which Louis is the oppressive tyrant and autocrat, reminiscent of the totalitarian leaders of the thirties, and Marlborough the courageous champion of human freedom, of religious and political choice, and of pluralism within the European order.

The contrast is not invariably so black and white. After Marlborough's first great victory over the French at Blenheim in South Germany, Churchill concedes that Louis XIV 'behaved with fortitude and dignity in the hour of misfortune'. And when he relates how the news of this French disaster was brought to Versailles, Churchill's animosity towards the 'Great King' modulates from rhetorical denunciation into some finely turned irony. Irony was one of Churchill's principle literary gifts. Here are two paragraphs which show Churchill at his most sophisticated in this manner of writing. The first paragraph is a quietly mocking account of the baroque culture of Versailles. The second is a gently managed deriding of a characteristic obsession with precedence and tittle-tattle at the court of the 'Great King' just before Marlborough's major victory is announced.

> The news of Blenheim came also to Versailles. A few days before the battle there had been a splendid evening fête at the Court. The most brilliant society in Europe was assembled, and the warm, delicious night favoured the festivities. Upon a triumphal car attended by warriors and nymphs the God of War was drawn past the daïs on which the Great King sat and Louis XIV displayed a lively pleasure in accepting his dutiful salute. There followed an allegorical representation of the state of Europe, in which all its rivers played their parts. The Thames, the Scheldt, the Rhine, the Meuse, the

> Neckar and also the Danube made their submission to the assumed pre-eminence of the Seine. The festival culminated in a prodigy of fireworks designed to bring home to the numerous and exalted company a vivid picture of modern war.
>
> An even more interesting topic occupied the Court. A dispute had arisen between two of the highest nobles upon their respective precedence. The historical argument ran back through centuries . . . The whole Court was divided upon the question, and a solemn tribunal had been appointed to resolve it. The keen interest of the King in the matter was well known, and his calm suspension of judgment admired . . . The imminence of the verdict kept all minds on tenterhooks. But one afternoon rumours began to spread of something ugly which had happened in Bavaria, and presently it was known that a courier from one of the armies in the field had been conducted by Chamillant to the King. They all had something else to talk about after that.

This last sentence is a good illustration of Churchill's powers with the sudden, blunt one-liner. Ironies have come to an end; the narrator takes a straightforward pleasure in the shock and consternation of the vain people in the tyrant's court. We can now return to the story of the hero and the villain.

Churchill establishes other characters in the story beside the two principle ones. First there is Barbara Villiers, who became John Churchill's lover when he, the son of an impoverished cavalier, was granted the favour of serving as a page at the court of the newly restored King Charles II. With the entrance of Barbara Villiers, *Marlborough* becomes Winston Churchill's first account of romantic love since that in his youthful novel *Savrola*. Barbara was also the King's mistress. 'She held Charles in intense fascination,' writes Churchill. 'She was a woman of exceeding beauty and charm, vital and passionate in an extraordinary degree. Her obsession with the handsome young page and the sexual triangle which she created were considered shocking even by the sophisticates of the restoration Court.' Churchill goes on: 'The intimacy of John and Barbara continued to cause Charles repeated annoyance, and their illicit loves, their adventures and escapades were among the most eminent scandals of the English court at this period.' Churchill is very much on the side of this older lady and her young lover, defending them against their critics and accounting for their relationship by telling us that 'the charms of thirty are rarely more effective than when exerted upon the impressionable personality of twenty-three'.

When John Churchill became a junior officer in the army, Barbara

Villiers, or the Duchess of Cleveland as she had by then become, very probably paid the money necessary for his commission. Mrs Manley, who, like her friend Jonathan Swift, was one of Marlborough's subsequent detractors, showed him in *The New Atlantis*, a scandal novel about the goings-on at the court of Charles II, to be a venal young man in this relationship, or worse. But Winston Churchill will have none of this. 'Why make of their romance a shameful scarecrow of mercenary vice?' Repudiating Mrs Manley as he repudiates other more distinguished critics of Marlborough such as Pope, Thackeray and Lord Macaulay, he launches into a belated polemic and some spirited literary criticism of her *roman à clef*, declaring, '*The New Atlantis* is a scandalous and indecent chronicle of the court of Charles II conceived in the mood of the *Decameron* or the memoirs of Casanova, but without the grace and sparkle which have redeemed these works.'

A contrast with John's colourful affair with Barbara, Duchess of Cleveland, is his relationship with Sarah Jennings, the love of his life, his wife and his political adviser and confidante, who also had come from humble origins to establish herself as a person of prime importance at court during the last years of the Stuart dynasty. John generally sought to set himself apart from the feuding factions of Tories and Whigs but Sarah, vividly characterised by Churchill, was very much a Whig. 'This handsome domineering woman, in the very centre of affairs, with her caustic tongue, her wit, her candour, and her common sense, was in herself a portent of the Age of Reason which had already dawned.' Characterful, wilful, pushy, sensuous, Sarah also had 'when roused, the temper of a devil'. Her love affair with John and their marriage, which was painfully delayed for some time by their poverty, had their ups and downs, but their relationship very evidently fascinates Churchill as an instance of a grand passion. Carefully modifying a cliché, he writes, 'It was a case of love, not at first sight indeed, but at first recognition. It lasted for ever . . .' John Churchill's life was entirely changed by 'the intensity of his passion for Sarah, before which adventure, ambition, and "lucre" alike lost their power'. Letting their love letters, or, at least, those of John to Sarah, speak for themselves, as well as evoking it in his own words Churchill conveys a strong sense of their turbulent, intense relationship. And he rounds on those who, like the sneering Macaulay, 'relegate' the importance of sexual love in a life. 'It is to him', deplores Churchill, nothing but 'a localized aberration which distorts judgement.' In the same sentence Churchill the biographer declares his own view of love, which is of 'a sublime passion which expresses and dominates all being'. Writing to his wife Clementine, while off researching the biography, Churchill again applied to Marlborough the word 'sublime', so current a word for the eighteenth-century prose stylists whom he so admired, Edmund Burke and Samuel Johnson. Of John Churchill Winston wrote confidingly to Clementine, 'It is only on the field and in his love for Sarah that he rises to the sublime.' In his very next sentence the former cavalry officer goes on to remind Clementine, 'Still Mars and Venus are two of the most important deities in the classical heaven.'

But for all the genuine admiration that Churchill feels for his hero's love and marriage, his four volumes overall show Marlborough often uneasy, dismayed, embarrassed or even compromised by his wife's doings as a court politician very close to Queen Anne. At the end of his life, when he retired from war and from politics, 'Sarah surrounded him with all kinds of quarrels'. 'She fought with her daughters, her in-laws, just about everyone she knew.' And the architect of Blenheim Palace, Queen Anne's great gift to Marlborough for his military successes against Louis XIV, Sarah attacked with particular enthusiasm. 'She fought Vanbrugh with zest and zeal.' Earlier in their marriage Sarah had turned violently on John himself, as Clementine once had on Winston, with accusations of infidelity. When their only son died, Sarah 'underwent not only grief, but those painful changes which mark the climacteric of a woman's life'. She became aggressive and violent towards her husband, as 'she persuaded herself that John had been unfaithful to her'. Even in the earliest days of the marriage, as Churchill describes it, Sarah led her husband a dance. John's unhappiness at this time, his biographer suggests, came from the intensity of his love. 'A man who cared less', Winston Churchill remarks, 'could have played this game of love with the sprightly Sarah much better than he.'

And, of course, one of the reasons for John's final humiliation, after all his spectacular successes as a general in the field and as the supreme commander of the international coalition of armies against Louis XIV, was his wife's loss of the friendship and favour of Queen Anne. Churchill the ex-novelist gives a vivid account of this friendship from the time when Anne was very much oppressed by her brother-in-law and sister, William and Mary, during the years they were on the throne before she herself became Queen and was able to give power to the close and supportive friends of her difficult times, John and Sarah Churchill. Given command of her armies, John achieved that sequence of brilliant military victories against Louis – Blenheim, Ramillies, Oudenarde and Malplaquet – which would constitute one of the great distinctions of her reign. Churchill is greatly interested in the Queen's character; 'what a woman she was, what a prince she was, and – what a Stuart!' He readily feels for her in various political situations and puts himself, as narrator, into her thoughts as she mulls over complicated political problems. He repudiates received and negative ideas of what Queen Anne was like. 'It is astonishing that most of our native historians have depicted Queen Anne as an obstinate simpleton, a stupid, weak creature, in the hands of her bedchamber women.' Nothing could be further from the truth, argues Churchill the revisionist historian, concluding that, 'On her throne she was as tough as Marlborough in the field.' He credits her with almost mystical powers, maintaining that 'she often interpreted in a shrewd and homely way to a degree almost occult what England needed and, still more, what England felt'. Assuming the editorial first person plural, Churchill says of his narrative strategy with regard to her and Marlborough, 'We portray her as a great Queen championed by a great Constable.' Elsewhere in the biography he ranks Queen Anne 'with Queen Elizabeth and the greatest sovereigns of the English line'.

For Churchill there is something tragic in the way in which in Anne's last years the association of the great Queen and the great Constable fell apart when Anne gradually rejected Sarah and finally replaced her with another bedchamber favourite, Mrs Masham. Sarah, galled and bitter, was driven ignominiously from Court. The new favourite facilitated the making of a new Tory administration headed by Harley and St John, who devoted themselves to driving Marlborough out of the leadership of the armies of a, by now, war-weary England. The sad story of the crumbling of Anne's two near life-long friendships ends, in Marlborough's case, in a kinkily degrading episode from which his biographer averts his eyes as being too sickening to dwell on. The two Tory leaders responsible for this awful nemesis of the great hero are, for Winston Churchill, entirely dishonourable and wicked men. Once again the biography becomes a moral tale. Harley and St John, the saboteurs of the career of England's great hero and the hero of free Europe, are in his view alike contemptible, St John, later Viscount Bolingbroke, especially so. Writing of their underhand abandonment of their associates in the Protestant alliance against Louis at the time of the Treaty of Utrecht, which brought the long war of the Spanish Succession to an end, Churchill says of these two Tory leaders: 'Just as they had obtained power . . . by a backstairs intrigue with the Queen, so they sought a peace by a greedy and treacherous desertion of their allies.' Their contemptible conduct, adds Churchill regretfully, entirely justifies 'the old French taunt "Perfidious Albion"'.

Churchill grants St John certain abilities, particularly literary ones. This 'roysterer and hard drinker', he concedes, 'had elevation of thought, breadth of view, and rare distinction in his use and comprehension of the English tongue'. He was both 'a patron of literature and a writer of high distinction'. And, of course, Bolingbroke's political writings such as *The Patriot King* and *Letters On The Study And Use Of History* are important documents in the history of Tory thought, having a very considerable influence on, for instance, Disraeli. But with all this said, Churchill still cannot conceal his loathing of this particular character in his highly dramatised biography. Bolingbroke is an 'unpurposed, unprincipled, miscreant adventurer', a man who at a critical juncture in the life of the century 'had neither the soul to decide nor the manhood to dare'. Churchill is astonished 'to find serious writers describing his actions as if they were deserving of impartial presentation'. For, however gifted, Bolingbroke is a man of 'wickedness and inherent degeneracy', 'a brilliant, fugitive rascal, prone to bully or grovel with equal facility according to circumstances or mood'.

Such clear-cut moral estimates are among the features of this biography that show it to be a work from between the wars. In these years there was a strong tendency for writers to see life in terms of absolutes of good and evil, the heroic and the villainous. Two examples are the 'Malatesta Cantos' of Ezra Pound and T.S. Eliot's play *Murder In the Cathedral*, which was written and produced while Churchill was at work on *Marlborough*. But if Churchill's moral assessments, like theirs, are unequivocal, even harsh, they are not simplistic. Bolingbroke, the subverter of the hero Marlborough, may be painted almost entirely black; Marlborough himself is not entirely white, but, rather, off-white. Churchill does concede certain peccadillos and faults. Above all, the great general and statesman, who had been brought up in poverty, loved money. Even when, late in life, he had amassed a great fortune, he always retained a keen eye for that extra perk. 'Anything in the nature of a perquisite stirred him . . .' But while Churchill allows such criticisms of his subject, it is without doubt his aim, and his achievement, as a biographer, to portray his ancestor as the leader of the forces of goodness and progress in one of the great and long crises in the history of the human spirit. It is a large and lofty theme but it is also convincingly actualised. What Churchill recurrently terms 'the actors' in his story are highly particularised human beings. But beyond these individual figures there is a larger narrative scale and movement to these thousands of pages. All of Europe is there. Marlborough and his friends and enemies are set at the centre of a process which ramifies to the very edges of the continent, from Portugal in the southwest to Sweden and Russia in the northeast, and from Scotland all the way southeast to the Turkish Empire. The larger historical process is made to show itself in different ways in different parts of John Churchill's long story; it is a matter of dynasties, of the politics of numerous royal families and generations, of the careers and characters of generals and princes, of diplomatic manoeuvring, of spying (Marlborough's 'secret sign' in the espionage activities which he organised was 'OO'), of party politics, of logistics, of weather, of strategies and tactics and of change of fortune in battles.

All these different kinds and levels of narrative are founded upon a formidable amount of scholarship and research. Churchill, we know, was assisted by several experts in different aspects of his narrative. But the learning is lightly worn and the wide-ranging contextual story never gets bogged down. One clear reason for this is that Churchill is always alive to the compelling analogy between the great struggle for control of Europe in the first decade or so of the 1700s and that later contest for domination in the second decade of the 1900s, the war that had been of such profound importance in Winston Churchill's own life. Marlborough's long war is 'the world war of the eighteenth century'. Driving back the enemy in 1704, 'The British troops felt the same thrills as rewarded their descendants when at the end of 1918 they drove the enemy before them through Belgium and the liberated provinces of France.' 'The strategic results of Bavaria joining France and Spain in 1702 resemble curiously in many points those that followed the accession of Turkey to Germany and Austria in 1914.' And Marlborough in his campaigns 'entered many French towns whose names have hallowed memories for our generation', such as Saint Quentin, Arras, Armentières. On one occasion Marlborough and his great comrade-in-arms Prince Eugene of Savoy, who had fought often against the Turks and helped to throw them back from the gates of Vienna, ride out together to assess the suitability of a particular terrain for a new manoeuvre against the French. They reject it as unsuitable and Churchill, with a curt concluding irony born of the terrible memories of this terrain, remarks, 'Our own experience at Passchendaele in 1917 in no way contradicts their impressions.'

The often poignant similarities between the two wars so distant from each other in time are not the only springs of emotion which animate Churchill's writing in this biography. His anger at what was going on in the thirties, the appeasement of Nazi Germany and the refusal of the Baldwin and Chamberlain governments and their supporters to face up to the growing danger, very obviously translates into anger against what Churchill saw as the inept, unprincipled government of Harley and St John, who brought the great Marlborough to that acutely painful moment of utter, and strangely perverse, humiliation. As he wrote his *Marlborough,* Churchill was also writing the series of regular newspaper articles, subsequently collected in the volume *Step By Step*, which sought desperately to alert his readership to the swiftly increasing threat from Hitler's Germany. At times these pieces have the urgency, the stridency even, of the prophet crying in the wilderness; they also have the unhesitating confidence of the writer of a moralised biography. The journalist who urges Britain to stand aside from involvement in the Spanish Civil War is also the biographer who remembers the suffering of Catalonia (to which just then George Orwell was paying his homage) as originating in the deplorable Treaty of Utrecht. 'The fate of the Catalans . . . even today plays its part in the internal affairs of Spain.' And the journalist who writes sarcastically about the ostrich-like attitudes and policies of Baldwin and MacDonald and the national governments of the thirties is also the biographer who, describing one of the nonentities who helped to undermine Marlborough, writes, 'We are witnessing an early eighteenth-century example of the process, familiar to twentieth-century democracy in every land, by which a pretentious, imposing mediocrity can be worked up into a national leader.'

What makes *Marlborough* such a powerful biography is, above all, the fact that Churchill feels, and feels with deep sympathy, for his subject. He is able to thrill to Marlborough's successes and to suffer with him in his moments of defeat, repudiation and rejection. Such feelings must always, to a greater or lesser extent, attach to the literary act known as biography. In Churchill's lengthy essay in the form, they are especially intense. Indeed they verge on the mystical. When he began writing the book Churchill told Keith Feiling, his son Randolph's tutor in history at Christchurch in Oxford, that he intended to write in a dramatic way so as to 'produce upon the mind of the reader the impersonation I wish to give'. To impersonate is one act of psychological transference for a biographer to undertake. But Churchill's recreating, re-living of Marlborough's life is made to seem even more thoroughgoing and overtly mystical when he writes of the biography to his cousin the present Duke of Marlborough, who was also, of course, of John Churchill's 'blood'. He speaks of his intention to raise from the dead 'this majestic shade'. Such an enterprise, he tells his cousin, 'is even, in a certain sense, a duty'. It is certainly for Churchill the writer an exciting ambition. 'To recall from the past this majestic shade and invest it with life and colour for the eyes of the twentieth century would be a splendid achievement.'

In Churchill's pages the first Duke of Marlborough is made to live in our minds because of the author's quickening feeling for him, his very evident admiration and love. Winston Churchill long ponders the many portraits of his hero and ancestor and observes of one of the paintings of John Churchill as a young man that 'there are disarming qualities in this beautiful countenance – strangely feminine, for so virile a nature, in its delicacy and charm'. The biographer also dwells on his ancestor's letters and the many qualities which these demonstrate. They also show Marlborough's powers as a writer of the English language. The letters, writes Churchill, 'plead for Marlborough's virtue, patriotism, and integrity as compulsively as his deeds vindicate his fame. Although no scholar, and for all his comical spelling, he wrote a rugged forceful English worthy of the Shakespeare on which his education was mainly founded.' An ability with, a delight in, the English language is one of the many bonds between Churchill and his subject. Such 'rugged forceful English' is something which Churchill himself often employs alongside his many eighteenth-century elegances of style. Here, to take just one instance, is Churchill's reply to the question asked on the death of Queen Anne, Who was her successor, George I? Churchill's one-sentence answer runs, 'A narrow, vindictive, humdrum German martinet, with dull brains, coarse tastes, crude appetites; a commonplace and ungenerous ruler, and a sluggish and incompetent commander in the field – that was all.'

Churchill the prose stylist admires another robust and skilled practitioner of English. Churchill the romantic sympathises quickly and profoundly with Marlborough the young lover. Churchill, the middle-aged victim of 'black dog', intense incapacitating depression, sympathises also with the middle-aged Marlborough's 'deepest gloom', 'black as night', that 'abysmal despair into which he was plunged in the two or three days before Oudenarde'. And Churchill the older writer, aged sixty-one in 1935, as he works away at his ever expanding labour of love, has a special feeling for the physical pains of Marlborough at the same age, on his last campaign, undergoing the danger of personally reconnoitring the enemy positions. 'We find him at sixty-one, in poor health, racked with earache and headache, after ten years of war, making these personal reconnaissances . . .' Above all we find Churchill, the man who had himself known humiliation, almost nauseated by his hero's worst moment of physical humiliation and indignity. As the friendship between Queen Anne and the Churchills weakened, John told his wife that there would come a moment when all that he, the elder statesman, could do would be to go down on his knees to the Queen in private, to abase himself before her, or, as he put it, with a strong hint of the physical unseemliness that this implied, to 'go on all fours' before her. Such an act of degradation actually took place. And Churchill the biographer is clearly and keenly disgusted by the thought and the image of it. The grovelling of the famous Duke, the great general and hero of all free Europe, this gross humiliation of a brave, perceptive and distinguished man is, declares

A FAMILY VISIT

"IT WAS A GREAT WORK, AND I WISH YOU COULD NOW ADD ANOTHER CHAPTER TO YOUR OWN CAREER."

Less than a year before the outbreak of the Second World War, Punch *shows Churchill visited by the subject of his latest book and encouraged by him to help repair Britain's political and military situation.*

Churchill, 'better suited to an Oriental setting than to a Christian land . . . Let us make haste to draw the curtain upon an unnatural spectacle.'

And what drove Marlborough on, past such ignominy and past all the lesser sufferings, betrayals and losses which he experienced in his life? What was the ultimate motivation of a man whom Churchill compares, recurrently, with Napoleon? The three simple phrases which Churchill offers in answer must surely be ones that explained his own unceasing efforts of a lifetime. His answer is: 'A page in history, a niche in Valhalla, and a good conscience to have used well the gifts which God had given: these must be the sole reward . . .' The undertaking of such elemental questions and answers about a life is a measure of the confidence of Churchill the biographer. The subject is a confirmation to the author. The life of Marlborough confirms Churchill's own highest aspirations in life as a humanist, a sceptic and an ironist. The aspirations are: to be remembered in history, to be associated with heroes, and to have used one's life and abilities properly and to the full.

CHAPTER NINE

Churchill's 'Brief Lives'

Towards the end of the thirties as he brought the immense biography to completion, Churchill had to face the possibility of a miserable ending to his political career just as his subject had done. Along with other parliamentary colleagues who opposed Neville Chamberlain's policy of appeasing Hitler, Churchill became aware of members of his constituency Conservative party calling for his deselection. Certain members of the party in West Essex called for him to be replaced as Member of Parliament by someone who would be more loyal to the official Conservative line in foreign policy. Still more threatening to his questionable prospects in the House of Commons at this time was yet one more major financial crisis in his life. In March 1938, when he was devoting himself wholeheartedly to his campaign against Nazism, he was shocked to find that the American investments on which he had relied since his partial recovery after his losses in the Great Crash had dramatically slumped in value. He discovered that his share account with his stockbrokers was in debt to the tune of some £18,000. The man who in less than eighteen months' time would again rejoin the government of his country as it approached the moment of its greatest danger now very seriously considered abandoning politics altogether. He would, and could, no longer donate his time and energies to his political struggle with the appeasers. He would devote himself to his writing which was, by far, his largest source of income. And he would sell Chartwell. He would also, as he told Clementine, follow up some 'great expectations of important business administrative employment', directorships which he would accept only as they accorded with his writing commitments and which would shield him from 'the truly stupendous task like Marlborough Vol. IV being finished in 4 or 5 months simply for current expenses'.

Matters deteriorated further; 'current expenses' became more difficult when, in April of that year, he was abruptly informed by the *Evening Standard*, one of Lord Beaverbrook's newspapers, that he was no longer wanted as a regular contributor. The reason for this had to do with the difference in views between Churchill and Beaverbrook on the European situation. But as Churchill now prepared himself to face his exclusion from political life, he was suddenly rescued by the efforts of his enthusiastic young supporter, Brendan Bracken. Using his extensive knowledge as a financial journalist, Bracken persistently but discreetly sought out those in the City who might help Churchill in his crippling financial difficulties. He finally succeeded in getting Sir Henry Strakosch, a long-established City financier, to guarantee Churchill's debts over the next four years. The seemingly doomed career of a former Home Secretary and Chancellor of the Exchequer was saved and so was Chartwell. This sudden upsurge in Churchill's personal fortunes was accompanied by one of his great publishing successes as an author, the collection of what he described to his publisher Thornton Butterworth as 'the short biographies' and which appeared under the title *Great Contemporaries*.

An appealing feature of the Marlborough biography is Churchill's ability to supply succinct and vivid character sketches. In *Great Contemporaries* Churchill's 'brief lives', like Aubrey's before them, show the same brilliant brevity in evoking a personality, often by centring on a saying, an image, or a very personal, Churchillian impression of the character. Admittedly Churchill did not know all the people whose lives he here relates in brief. His account of Trotsky is an essay in depreciation, always ironic and sometimes sarcastic, rather than a biography. The short study of Franklin Delano Roosevelt, whom Churchill, at the time of writing, had not yet met, is chiefly a series of nervous reservations about what Churchill regarded as some of the left-wing policies in the President's series of programmes, the New Deal. And the piece on Hitler is an uneasy pondering of possible German actions in the future as the essay on Hindenburg, the German commander in the First World War, is a reminder of the recent German past. But these four items are not what makes this collection of brief lives the unusual but distinguished work of prose that it is. These four but serve to remind us of a larger historical context, to which his other, more compelling and vivid subjects, men whom Churchill actually knew, belonged.

It is Churchill's personal knowledge of each of his subjects, his personal insights into and feeling about them that vitalise each essay and make the reader feel that he has been in close contact with the characterful and forceful personalities whom Churchill here remembers and resurrects. They are a very varied group of men, and they are all men. Like the portrait busts of the sculptor Jacob Epstein, they show us some of the chief *dramatis personae* in the social and political life of the first third and more of this century. Churchill begins with Lord Rosebery, the last Liberal Prime Minister of the nineteenth century, and a last representative of an older order, a wealthy racehorse-owner and twice the winner, during his premiership, of the Derby; also an 'epicure, bookworm, literary critic, magpie collector of historical relics, appreciative owner of veritable museums of art treasure . . .' 'He was', Churchill continues, 'one of the first Whig nobles who as a young man embraced the Liberal and democratic conceptions of the later nineteenth century.' More important still for this biographer-in-brief: 'Lord Rosebery was probably my father's greatest friend.' The notion of his father's generation is one of the great themes and touchstones that helps to organise this collection of character portraits. In late middle age Winston Churchill is still intensely fascinated by his father's friends and contemporaries, the late-Victorians who had formed the social and political background, and the impress, of his own youth. Admiringly, Churchill exclaims, 'How these Victorians busied themselves and contended about minor things! What long, brilliant, impassioned letters they wrote each other about refined personal and political issues of which the modern Juggernaut progression takes no account.' He characterises their generational position further by adding, 'They never had to face, as we have done, and still do, the possibility of national ruin.' 'Rosebery flourished in an age of great men and small events.'

Another of the 'great men' of this late-Victorian generation was the much more left-wing Liberal, John Morley, Gladstone's biographer and, in old age, the young Churchill's close and highly respected Cabinet colleague in Asquith's Liberal government in Edwardian times. Churchill's portrait of him is marked by admiration and even awe. 'From 1908 onwards my seat in the Cabinet was next to his. Six years of constant, friendly and to me stimulating propinquity!' Churchill evidently sees much of himself in this Liberal elder statesman. The following words about John Morley could so easily be applied to Churchill himself: he 'was always a fascinating companion, a man linked with the past . . . the representative of great doctrines, an actor in historic controversies, a master of English prose, a practical scholar, a statesman-author . . .' Also, and again importantly, Morley was 'the friend and contemporary of my father'. Such men, and others of approximately that generation, Joseph Chamberlain, Arthur Balfour and Charles Stewart Parnell, supply standards of eminence, charisma and culture against which Churchill tacitly measures the men of a later time, his own.

The story of Parnell's leadership of the Irish struggle for Home Rule in the late nineteenth century is told by Churchill with much trenchancy and dramatic power. Parnell's love affair with Kitty O'Shea, the wife of one of his parliamentary followers, and Parnell's eventual social and political disgrace and his abandonment by both Gladstone and the Irish Catholic Church are presented in sentences of brief simplicity that make a familiar story suspenseful and affecting. Churchill's swift evocation of character and episode are such that his comparison of his story with some famous story in Greek literature comes, in his final paragraph, as in no way inappropriate. He concludes, 'Such is the tale which comprised all the elements of Greek tragedy. Sophocles or Euripides could have found in it a theme sufficient to their sombre taste.' There is no evidence that the young Winston Churchill ever met Parnell. But the source of the vital fascination with the man and the drama and the romance in Churchill's telling of the tale must surely have come from his father Lord Randolph's talk during Winston's boyhood.[1] For Parnell was one of the Irish leaders with whom Lord Randolph, 'Leader of the Tory Democracy', was, as Winston Churchill notes, in 'close and deep relation'. This beautifully managed brief life of Parnell shows every sign of being a story long known, mulled over since childhood and then set down unassumingly by a narrator who has the confidence and the literary skill to let the tale, with all its inherent power, speak for itself.

Filial piety is not the only energising force in these 'brief biographies.' Certainly Churchill, a writer with always something of the dramatist in him, takes a great pleasure in putting himself into the minds and feelings of others. As he contemplates the German Kaiser exiled to Holland on that historic day in November 1918, Churchill quickly repudiates the simplistic 'Hang the Kaiser' attitude of British popular opinion and imagines himself into Kaiser Wilhelm's situation, beginning his biographical sketch with the question, 'What should I have done in his position?' His answers lead to the conclusions that the Kaiser was less the cause, and more the consequence and the victim, of certain simple facts of German life, 'the well-crunched parade-ground

[1] In the portrait Churchill also mentions Mrs O'Connor, the wife of an Irish member from whom 'when I was a boy', 'I heard many tales and received many vivid pictures of Parnell and his rise and fall'.

of Potsdam' and the inherent subservience of the German people 'to the barbaric idea of autocracy'. Churchill the biographer-dramatist develops his view by contrasting two images; the Kaiser, whom Churchill as a British cabinet minister had visited at the German army manoeuvres of 1906 and then again of 1908, the resplendent emperor entering the city of Breslau, riding 'his magnificent horse at the head of a squadron of cuirassiers, wearing their white uniform and eagle-crested helmet', and then the second image, from just twelve years later, of a 'broken man . . . hunched in a railway carriage, hour after hour, at a Dutch frontier station awaiting permission to escape as a refugee . . .' Churchill then dwells on the Kaiser's personal mediocrity, his 'lack of understanding, sense of proportion' and the blatant lack 'of literary capacity' in his memoirs. Churchill concludes: 'It is shocking to reflect that upon the word or nod of a being so limited there stood attentive and obedient for thirty years the forces which, whenever released, could devastate the world. It was not his fault; it was his fate.'

Two other essays in empathising, in 'feeling for' his human subjects, are about the two great French leaders of the Great War, the soldier Marshal Foch and the statesman Clemenceau. In characterising the French general who risked the massive and, as it proved, decisive attack upon the Germans in the summer of 1918, Churchill resorts to mystical notions which surely tell of himself as well as of his subject. Foch, Churchill suggests, was a 'predestined being'. Humiliated by France's defeat by the Germans in 1870, Foch went on 'to nourish within himself those deep and in some respects mystic forces which were the resultants of his pain'. These become features of Foch's personality which in Churchill's description of them require, what is for us today, some unusual and elemental phrasing. Foch's last daring onslaught upon the Germans was not just 'one of the greatest deeds of war . . . which history has recorded', it was also an example of 'fortitude of soul'. Such a profound and powerful phrase is a part of that earned elevation of style which on occasion conveys Churchill's admirations in these biographical essays. In his moving account of Lawrence of Arabia, for instance, Churchill remarks, simply and unaffectedly, 'He looked what he was, one of nature's greatest princes.' And when Churchill's hero Clemenceau took over France in early 1918, when its government was panicky and despairing and its battered armies mutinous, the coming to power of this veteran of nearly fifty years of French politics is described by Churchill with adjectives which become poetic but which remain entirely convincing. Clemenceau at the beginning of 1918, says Churchill, was 'doubted by many, dreaded by all, but doom-sent, inevitable'.

A special bond between the biographer-in-brief and 'The Tiger' Clemenceau, and also Colonel Lawrence and John Morley and Lord Rosebery, is that they, like he, were all writers as well as statesmen. Churchill the literary portraitist is especially comfortable with men involved with power and action who are also men of letters. An important reason for Churchill's admiration for Rosebery, for instance, is that he was 'one of those men of affairs who add to the unsure prestige of a minister and the fleeting successes of an orator the more enduring achievements of literature'. Churchill singles out for praise Rosebery's 'appreciations of great poets and writers like Burns and Stevenson' and his letters, which 'are alive with Byronic wit and colour'. In the portrait of Asquith, the Prime Minister who first gave the young Churchill major political office, the biographer remembers his former boss as a connoisseur of English, as someone by whom 'repetition, verbiage, rhetoric, false argument, would be impassively but inexorably put aside'. Looking back on those holiday times in the Eastern Mediterranean, on board the *Enchantress*, Churchill the autodidact recalls how Asquith the classical scholar from Balliol College, Oxford, 'basked in the sunshine and read Greek. He fashioned with deep thought impeccable verses in complicated metre, and recast in terser form classical inscriptions which displeased him.' Churchill could not hope to emulate Asquith in Latin and Greek; nevertheless the classics supply some important points of reference in these Plutarchian accounts of men and writers. T.E. Lawrence's *The Seven Pillars of Wisdom*, for instance, 'this treasure of English literature', which 'ranks with the greatest books ever written in the English language', is compared very favourably with the *Commentaries* of Julius Caesar. Churchill as literary critic also places it alongside English classics of the standing of *The Pilgrim's Progress, Robinson Crusoe* and *Gulliver's Travels*.

Another writer to appear in this gallery of small portraits is George Bernard Shaw, whom Churchill declares to be 'the greatest living master of letters in the English-speaking world'. But the essay as a whole actually contains more equivocation about Shaw than this grand phrase in the final sentence would suggest. Churchill, writing again as a literary critic, reproaches Shaw for at times writing 'bombinating nonsense' and for making some very faulty literary judgements. 'In a moment when his critical faculty is evidently slumbering, he even ranks William Morris with Goethe.' And Shaw's political views Churchill cannot take seriously. Churchill recalls his first meeting with Shaw around the turn of the century when, 'My mother, always in agreeable contact with artistic and dramatic circles, took me to luncheon with him.' At that time the young cavalry officer had bitterly resented an article by Shaw mocking the activities of the British army. Later on in Churchill's life the two men had met again from time to time and discussed the Irish problem and also socialism. Shaw's politics are such that Churchill can only portray him as 'the jester'. Shaw's socialism and his sympathy for the Soviet Union and for Stalin elicit from Churchill passages which answer Shavian wit in kind. Churchill focused on Shaw's good-will visit to Russia in the company of 'his co-delegate or comrade', Lady Astor, the American multimillionairess who was the first woman to be elected to the House of Commons. Churchill pauses to savour and to enjoy the question of what the Russians made of this two-person team of the 'aged Jester, with his frosty smile and safely invested capital' and the fabulously wealthy lady who was the 'leader of fashionable society and of advanced feminist democracy'. 'What a pair.' What 'a merry harlequinade!' But then, 'The Russians have always been fond of circuses and travelling shows.' 'And here was the World's most famous intellectual Clown and Pantaloon in one, and the charming Columbine of the capitalist pantomime.'

But then abruptly the tone of Churchill's essay changes from the light-hearted to the sombre. 'Well was it said that the genius of comedy and tragedy are essentially the same.' And now Churchill moves on from Shaw and Lady Astor as a comedy team to Russia under Stalin as a tragedy. The tone is now one of indignation and then of denunciation. This ready hostility to Bolshevik Russia, a radical, even rabid, hostility, is an emotion that recurs in these brief biographies. The Russian revolution and its consequences are for Churchill among the main causes of the destabilising of that sure world order which was one of the unquestioned assumptions of 'my father's generation'. The portrait which has most to do with this, for Churchill, supremely tragic event is of the least remembered of the figures whose life stories are told in this collection; it is the brief biography of Boris Savinkov, a Russian novelist and Nihilist. In his novel *The Pale Horse*, written under a pseudonym, Savinkov depicted his numerous activities in Czarist times as a Nihilist terrorist; his missions included several assassinations, including that of the Grand Duke Serge. But when the revolution came, Savinkov was no more content with Lenin's regime that he had been with the Czar's. He had thrown in his lot with Kerensky and his revolutionary government, but when this was pushed aside by the Bolsheviks Savinkov associated himself with the resistance to the new Communist regime led by the Czarist officers who led the White Russian cause, General Denikin and Admiral Kolchak. Savinkov was their representative and spokesman at the treaty-making at Versailles in 1919 and it was here, in the summer of that year, that Churchill, a very active member of Lloyd George's coalition government, first met him. Churchill was immediately intrigued. 'I had never seen a Russian Nihilist except on the stage, and my first impression was that he was singularly well cast for the part.' Churchill goes on to characterise the man in a sequence of carefully and precisely worded sentences; he was clearly impressed by him. 'His being was organised upon a theme. His life was devoted to a cause. That cause was the freedom of the Russian people. In that cause there was nothing he would not dare or endure. He had not even the stimulus of fanaticism. He was that extraordinary product – a Terrorist for moderate aims.' 'The Czar and Lenin seemed to him the same things expressed in different terms, the same tyranny in different trappings, the same barrier in the path of Russian freedom.'

As the White Russian resistance to the Bolsheviks grew weaker, Savinkov was given certain assurances which lured him back to Russia. But the promises made to him were not kept once he had returned. He was arrested and held in jail. 'Tormented in his prison cell with false hopes and shifting promises, squeezed by the most subtle pressures, he was at length induced to write his notorious letter of recantation and to proclaim the Bolshevik Government as the liberator of the world.' Shortly afterwards Boris Savinkov either committed suicide or was shot. In his story of the man Churchill dwells on an image of him at Chequers, where, accompanied by Churchill, he had gone to discuss the situation in Russia with the Prime Minister, Lloyd George. The scene remained vividly in Churchill's mind down to the Welsh hymns which a band of Welsh singers had come to Chequers to perform for the Prime Minister and which, that Sunday, 'they sang in the most beautiful manner'. In the conversations that day in the very early twenties the Prime Minister had been optimistic about the Russian revolution. Savinkov had not. And, in Churchill's view, Savinkov had been right. And the fact and the circumstances of his death were for Churchill an indictment of the Soviet regime. The last sentence of Churchill's portrayal of him has a sombre, even tragic, tone as, while allowing for his subject's failings, he commends his particular heroism, for 'with all the stains and tarnishes few men tried more, gave more, dared more and suffered more for the Russian people'.

The first edition of *Great Contemporaries* ended with an essay on King George V and his reign which gave to the collection a sense of, to use Churchill's phrase in the Preface, 'historical narrative', of a sequence of portraits illustrating the last fifty years or so of recent history. The second and extended edition of the book a year later had far more essays and concluded with one entitled 'Roosevelt From

THE WELLS OF TRUTH

H.G. Wells was a writer whom Churchill admired and with whom he corresponded over many years. But Churchill was greatly angered by the sympathy which Wells felt for Lenin and the Bolshevik regime in Russia. This cartoon shows the ferocity of Churchill's hostility to Wells's pro-Soviet book Russia in the Shadows.

Afar', which ended the collection with more of an emphasis upon possibilities for, and questions about, the future. But in both editions the horrific shock of the Russian revolution remains a recurrent emotion and reference; Churchill's strong anti-Soviet feelings were a conspicuous feature of his politics as well as of his writings during the thirties. And in 1939, about eighteen months after *Great Contemporaries* first appeared, a publisher invited Churchill to develop his views in a book to be entitled 'Europe Since The Revolution'. Churchill was taken with the idea and signed a contract. But before he could proceed very far with the project, there at last came that long-hoped-for summons to rejoin the government which marked both the end of his decade in the political wilderness and the vindication of his long opposition to the appeasement of Germany. Five years later, in 1944, when Churchill had long since become Prime Minister of Britain and ever more famous throughout the world, the publishers asked for the manuscript to be delivered. Churchill refused. 'My whole outlook is changed,' he replied. 'The synopsis which was a living thing then, is now dead. . . . Am I to bring up the horrors of the Russian Revolution? . . . To ask me to do this, is a thing that no reasonable person would do. . . . I certainly should not be on speaking terms with Stalin if I wrote the things I would have written in time of peace.'

The call to become Prime Minister in May 1940 was to change his life and his outlook radically. The seeming failure and spent force who had been accustomed to divide his time between Chartwell, Westminster and the Mediterranean villas and yachts of his wealthy friends suddenly had an entirely new life. The unexpected, the unthinkable had happened. Events had proved Chamberlain and the appeasers to be entirely in the wrong. Winston Churchill was suddenly the leader of a Britain threatened with physical destruction. He established himself as a Prime Minister, he became leader of the once hostile Conservative party, he gained a reputation as the greatest orator in English of this century. A man now in his late sixties, he flew about the world in aircraft which by today's standards were uncomfortable and unreliable, in order to meet with those who had superseded the members of the Chartwell set as his most important human relationships. An important part, humanly as well as politically, of his historic premiership, were friendships with two men whom he had previously never met, President Franklin Delano Roosevelt and that figure from the demonology of his writings of the twenties and thirties, with whom he had never thought to be on speaking terms, Joseph Stalin.

On his return to government, initially as First Lord of the Admiralty and then as Prime Minister, Churchill tried to continue with his contractual obligations as a writer. But the pressures of wartime politics and administration soon stopped this effort. For five years and more Churchill's writing was virtually in abeyance while as a national and then as a world leader he took on those immense responsibilities which gave him a heroic stature unimaginable, even to himself, during the years before 1939. But the career of the writer was by no means at an end. Out of those historic activities in the years between 1939 and 1945 there came one last large literary work which was in terms of history and of English literature entirely unprecedented and extraordinary. It was the story of a world war related evocatively by one of its leading participants, a story in which other chief participants are remembered and realised and presented, in repeated portraits, by a vital and highly practised literary imagination.

CHAPTER TEN

The Second World War in Deeds Then Words

For Churchill it was a moving experience on that September day in 1939 to return as First Lord to Admiralty House in Whitehall, which almost a quarter of a century before he had been compelled to leave with his political career in ruins. When he saw again the famous Boardroom, the octagonal table and the sea charts of the world stored behind the wooden panelling, he was, a senior naval officer recalled, 'filled with emotion'. Even a fortnight later, when he was starting to ponder a naval attack on the Norwegian coast at Narvik in order to impede supplies of Swedish iron ore routed to Nazi Germany, Churchill's mind still dwelled on his old problematical colleagues, the admirals of the First World War: Fisher, Beatty and Jellicoe. And of all the scores of poems he knew by heart it was one by Thomas Moore, 'Oft in the Stilly Night', that came most recurrently into his mind. As he remembered the old days in that Admiralty building, the now 65-year-old Churchill recited aloud Moore's lines:

I feel like one
Who treads alone
Some banquet-hall deserted,
Whose lights are fled,
Whose garlands dead,
And all but he departed.

In those early months at the Admiralty during what was called the 'phoney war', Churchill struggled to continue to work on his commitments as a writer, as he had when he had last held ministerial office as Chancellor of the Exchequer. Even as late as early 1940 he tried to carry on with his *History of the English-Speaking Peoples*, the most team-written of all his works. One research assistant, F.W. Deakin, though in training with the Oxfordshire Yeomanry Anti-Tank Regiment, worked away on the chapters on the Victorian age. Maurice Ashley drafted an account of Oliver Cromwell and a young Oxford scholar, Alan Bullock, years later a biographer of Hitler, prepared sections on Canada, Australia and New Zealand. But work pressures and worries at the Admiralty intensified as the Norwegian venture ran into difficulties and the Chamberlain government faced increasing criticism. And then came that historic day in May of 1940 when Chamberlain, deserted in a House of Commons vote by a significant number of Conservative members, resigned the Prime Ministership and King George VI invited Churchill to take his place. From then Churchill's writing career was virtually suspended for some five years as his life moved to Downing Street and to his official country residence at Chequers, where, surrounded by advisers and secretaries and responding to an unceasing flow of visitors, he took over the government of Britain at a time of unprecedented crisis. But even in those shocking, disastrous early months of his premiership which saw France capitulate to the Germans, which saw the British army barely escape from France at Dunkirk and which saw the beginning of the Battle of Britain in the air, and of the threat of sudden invasion by sea, there was created that quick succession of letters, minutes, directions and telegrams, all of a markedly literary quality, which would later serve as the basis of that history of the war which would be unique in being written by one of the leading participants in it. 'Never has the world had the history of a gigantic war written by the Napoleon himself,' remarked Admiral Lord Louis Mountbatten when Churchill set to work in 1945. But the book had long been pondered in Churchill's mind, even as the events it describes were occurring. Even before the London Blitz was over Churchill was already, so he told his dinner guests at Chequers, planning to 'write a book on the war, which he had already mapped out in his mind chapter by chapter'. During the painful losses and defeats of the first years of his premiership Churchill was still mindful of his fellow writers. Around the time of the humiliating loss of Singapore to the Japanese, Churchill read and enjoyed two novels, *Sergeant Lamb of the Ninth* and *Proceed Sergeant Lamb*, by Siegfried Sassoon's friend, Robert Graves. Though at the time involved in delicate and protracted negotiations with the American ambassador, Churchill took time to write to Graves from

Chequers, congratulating him on his 'wonderful gift of recalling' and adding, 'I am a great lover of narrative, in which you excel.'

Churchill's famous inspirational speeches to Parliament and to radio audiences during 'their finest hour' also showed Churchill's great love for and knowledge of literature. John Colville was one of the duty secretaries who in the early years of the war accompanied Churchill on his restless round from Downing Street to the country houses at Chequers and Ditchley, to inspections of defence installations on the south coast. Colville also went with Churchill to see such terrible sights as the bombed-out streets of the East End of London and the fires burning on Plymouth Docks, with the makeshift coffins of the many dead piled high in the one remaining harbour warehouse, where they could be seen by the wounded, the maimed and those in agony receiving stopgap medical attention on the debris-littered stone floor. Colville noted in his diary how Churchill tried to reassure these and others in similarly appalling conditions, and how at such times Churchill began working out the celebrated speeches delivered in the House of Commons and on BBC radio. The Prime Minister, Colville remembered, continually recalled to himself quotations and lines of poetry which he would continue to murmur to himself, repeating them in different ways and placing them in different contexts. Observing Churchill's habit of referring to literature for wisdom, for strength and for oratory, Colville commented, the Prime Minister 'fertilizes a line of poetry or a phrase for weeks'.

One of Churchill's favourite literary recourses at the dismal time of the prospect of having to 'fight on the beaches' was to some stanzas from the Victorian poet Arthur Clough. These included lines about the movement of the tide which for Churchill seemed well to express long-term hope in a time of immediate, short-term discouragement and frustration.

> For while the tired waves, vainly breaking,
> Seem here no painful inch to gain,
> Far back, through creeks and inlets making,
> Comes silent, flooding in, the main.

One of the occasions Churchill read these lines was in a radio speech in April 1941 after he had visited Bristol in the aftermath of a major air raid and had seen the city burning and dead bodies being brought out from under the deep rubble. The poem helped to sustain Churchill, who had seen so many wars, in the face of 'devastation such as I had never thought possible'. The terrible air war could also prompt Churchill to employ poetry more lightheartedly. When he was visited by President Roosevelt's emissaries, Anthony Biddle and Averell

Harriman, early in 1941 he took the two Americans up on to the roof of the Air Ministry to view a German bombing attack and the activities of the British fighters, and he quoted to them Alfred, Lord Tennyson's prophetic vision of air warfare from the poem 'Locksley Hall'. They were the same lines about future air combat which Churchill had quoted in his essay 'Fifty Years Hence' in *Thoughts and Adventures*.

> For I dipt into the future, far as human eye could see,
> Saw the Vision of the world, and all the wonder that would be;
> . . . .
> Heard the heavens fill with shouting, and there rain'd a ghastly dew
> From the nations' airy navies grappling in the central blue;

For the writer Prime Minister the English literary tradition was an important psychological resource in the difficult, often agonising, early years of the war. As Churchill proceeded with his chief diplomatic ambition, that of making Roosevelt's America into a sympathiser and then into an ally of beleaguered Britain, it was to this feature of Churchill's mind that the President responded when, encouragingly, in the spring of 1941 he sent Churchill some lines by the American poet Longfellow. The President wrote just a year before Pearl Harbor. 'I think this verse applies to your people as it does to us.'

> Thou, too, sail on, O Ship of State!
> Sail on, O Union, strong and great!
> Humanity with all its fears,
> With all the hope of future years,
> Is hanging breathless on thy fate!

Characteristically, Churchill chose the 1941 meeting of the American Booksellers Association as one opportunity for rallying public support in the United States to the side of Britain. In the message which he took upon himself to send to the annual conference of this body he stressed the issue of free speech which the war raised. He spoke of man's need to have access to 'The mighty power of the spirit in the word'. And he reminded his listeners of the historical importance of the freedom to read for the 'English-speaking peoples who from writers living and dead gather courage and constancy to strengthen us . . .'

Once the United States had entered the war, Churchill's Prime Ministership changed markedly; the story becomes, in considerable part, a travelogue. He journeyed first to Newfoundland and soon after to Washington DC to confer with the President. And then in draughty, or else overheated, noisy aircraft he flew via North Africa to Iran and southern Russia, to visit Stalin in Moscow. In January 1943 as advantage in the war began just perceptibly to shift to the Allied side, Churchill had another of his meetings with President Roosevelt, this time on the northwest coast of Africa, at Casablanca. When the conference was over, Churchill persuaded his new, and soon very dear, friend Franklin Roosevelt to accompany him to nearby Marrakesh, where Churchill did a painting of what he called 'the most lovely spot in the whole world'. It was a view of the peaks of the Atlas Mountains tinted one moment red, another moment purple, and by any and all shades in between, by the setting sun. Churchill had visited the place in the thirties and now he insisted that Roosevelt, whose legs had been crippled by polio, be carried up to the roof of the villa where their party was staying, in order to see the spectacular view. Lord Moran, the doctor who now always accompanied Churchill on his journeys, remembered seeing Roosevelt's servants improvise a chair with their arms to carry the President up the narrow, winding stone stairs to the roof, 'his paralysed legs dangling down like the limbs of a ventriloquist's dummy, limp and flaccid'. Once on that roof top at Marrakesh the two leaders, who had come so quickly to a deep affection for each other, paused for a good while to survey the spectacular beauty before them. It was a memorable moment in an important friendship. It was also an occasion on which Churchill's artistic talent asserted itself. For after the President had gone, Churchill set to and, putting aside all his political, military and administrative worries, worked at a landscape painting of the mountains. It was his one and only painting of all the war years.

Lord Moran became an important and a permanent member of Churchill's travelling entourage as the incessant journeyings began seriously to jeopardise the Prime Minister's health. Before the war ended he had two heart attacks and a very serious case of pneumonia. Yet he was always quick to ridicule Moran's advice and caution and to involve himself in the actualities of the fighting. After the allied landings on the French coast on D-day in 1944, Churchill was keen to visit the most advanced positions of the British forces, now led by General Montgomery, who had made himself famous for his victories over Rommel in the war in the North African desert. When British troops crossed the Rhine Churchill again insisted on being in the forefront with them. Agreeing to Churchill's demand, Montgomery, already looking ahead to his writing of his own memoirs, informed Churchill, the vastly more experienced writer, that 'I shall ask you to write a Chap[ter] for my book!!!' As the allied armies pushed on into Germany and then met up with the Russians advancing from the East, Churchill's great fame as a world leader and world hero began to have what was to be a rapidly escalating effect upon his standing as a writer; in April 1945 he was able to tell Clemmie, who at that time was Stalin's honoured guest in Moscow, that the film rights for the as yet uncompleted and unpublished 'History of the English-Speaking Peoples' had been sold to Alexander Korda and 'the cheque is on its way to the bank'.

Some three months later, very shortly after the great personal and national triumph of V-E Day, Churchill suffered one of the great blows of his life when he, and the Conservative party which he led, was decisively defeated in the General Election. After more than five years at the centre of power and decision-making that ramified throughout the world, he was suddenly little more than a private citizen again; media attention, the day-to-day administration of the country were now assumed by Churchill's successor, the new Labour Prime Minister, Clement Attlee. Churchill's daughter Mary has feelingly recalled her seventy-year-old father's sudden and devastating lack of function and purpose in July, 1945. 'The Map Room was deserted; the Private Office empty; no official telegrams; no "red boxes". After years of intense activity, for Winston now there was a yawning hiatus.' Churchill's second-in-command in the Conservative party, Anthony Eden, noted sadly in his diary Churchill's agonising desolation: '. . . he feels the blow heavily and his pride is hurt. He said, "it hurts more like a wound which becomes more painful after the first shock".' Clementine Churchill wrote unhappily about the terrible strain the great electoral defeat had laid upon their marriage. 'I cannot explain how it is but in our misery we seem, instead of clinging to each other, to be always having scenes. I'm sure it's all my fault, but I'm finding life more than I can bear. He is so unhappy and that makes him very difficult.' After the years of often luxurious world travel, the Churchills had now to face the shortages and austerity of post-war Britain. Clementine, worried about starting to repair Chartwell after five years of virtual abandonment and neglect, continued in her letter to Mary, 'we shan't have a car. We are being lent one. We are learning how rough and stoney the world is.'

One of the ways in which Churchill brought himself out of the depression caused by his loss of the Prime Ministership was his resumption of his literary career. Clearly his memoirs of the war promised to be an extremely valuable property in the book trade. In late August 1945, when Churchill was having dinner at Claridges with his son Randolph and Brendan Bracken, the talk turned to the question of who should be Churchill's agent in making the complicated legal and contractual arrangements for publishing the memoirs worldwide. Churchill was both anxious and highly sensitive about this matter and there occurred one of the terrible recurrent rows between father and son, which built into a noisy scene and which ended with Randolph standing up and striding angrily from the public dining room. But the problem of who was to administer the forthcoming massive literary enterprise did not go away. Eventually, in January of the following year, when Churchill was in the United States and about to make the famous speech in Fulton, Missouri, about the Russian creation of an 'iron curtain' in Europe, he invited Emery Reves, his literary agent in the thirties, then working in Europe but now based in America, to come and see him. A Hungarian Jew who had studied in Germany, France and Switzerland, Emery Reves (formerly Revesz) had in 1930 founded an international literary agency which came to specialise in promoting anti-fascist writing. Writers for whom Reves acted included Albert Einstein, Austen Chamberlain, Anthony Eden and the French prime ministers Leon Blum and Paul Reynaud. Churchill still remembered gratefully the efforts of Emery Reves to place his newspaper articles during the thirties, when Churchill's political and financial position had been difficult. Feeling excited and privileged by Churchill's invitation that January day of 1946, Reves hastened from Chicago to Miami, to lunch with his former author, flying the last lap of the journey in a British Embassy plane. Churchill told Reves that he had not forgotten what he had done for him before the war and asked him to act for him now. Reves, through Lord Camrose, the proprietor of the *Daily Telegraph* and a financial adviser to Churchill, was finally to buy all the foreign rights for Churchill's work in progress on the Second World War.

As Churchill's agent, Reves would have the delicate task of pointing out to him what various editors saw as the literary inadequacies of what the author regarded as the absolutely final draft of his first volume of his story of the war, *The Gathering Storm*. The conclusion of all the years of writing and agenting the memoirs was to be marked by the very elderly Churchill's strong sentimental attachment to Reves's then lover, later his wife, Wendy Russell. On many occasions in his later years Churchill would be a guest in their villa on the French Riviera. Known as La Pausa, the villa had been originally built by the Duke of Westminster for the couturier Coco Chanel. Emery Reves bought it out of the handsome rewards of being Churchill's agent in the late forties and the fifties. Wendy's intense feeling for Churchill began in her sense of gratitude for what his retaining of Emery had meant for their prosperity and wellbeing. When he first went to stay at La Pausa Churchill wrote home to Clementine, saying of Wendy, 'She persists in begging me to stay, saying in her husband's presence that I have done everything for him and that they can never repay etc.'

During the next few years Churchill's relationship with Wendy grew in closeness and strength of feeling before coming to its emotionally difficult climax. But the problematical finale of Churchill's involvement with the Reveses still lay some years in the future when, in late 1947, Churchill completed the first volume of his war memoirs and sent it on to Emery.

Reves was uneasy about the manuscript and wrote to Churchill suggesting that a considerable amount of rewriting was necessary. Churchill's title for the story of the twenty years prior to his assumption of the premiership was 'The Downward Path'. Emery Reves thought this unattractively negative and suggested instead 'The Gathering Storm', an idea which Churchill accepted. Reves also thought that there were 'too many documents, letters and quotes from speeches in the text'. He thought that 'the narrative is so dramatic, so exciting, that one resents the many interruptions, and the average reader will certainly skip . . .' Churchill was irritated by such criticisms. Weary from all the work involved in his two-fold career as writer and leader of the opposition in Parliament, he was loath to act on them. But the text as it was published remains vulnerable to Reves' objections. The story does often get bogged down in detailed documentation such as statistics and tables. The result is that, along with the subsequent volumes, the work is likely to recommend itself as a totality only to those with specialist interest in the complex unfolding of the Second World War. For the general reader the work only becomes alive when Churchill evokes a particular occasion or a particular person of importance in what is the distinctively autobiographical strand in the narrative. An instance is his paragraph describing his feelings on that May night in 1940 after the King had asked him to form a government. His evocation of his sudden sense of calm at that climatic moment is finely done; the vocabulary is quietly ordinary and unpretentious and the syntax characterised chiefly by simple sentences.

> During these last crowded days of the political crisis my pulse had not quickened at any moment. I took it all as it came. But I cannot conceal from the reader of this truthful account that as I went to bed at about 3 a.m., I was conscious of a profound sense of relief. At last I had the authority to give directions over the whole scene. I felt as if I were walking with destiny, and all my past life had been but a preparation for this hour and for this trial. Eleven years in the political wilderness had freed me from ordinary Party antagonisms. My warnings over the last six years had been so numerous, so detailed, and were now so terribly vindicated, that no one could

gainsay me. I could not be reproached either for making the war or with want of preparation for it. I thought I knew a good deal about it all, and I was sure I should not fail. Therefore, although impatient for the morning, I slept soundly and had no need for cheering dreams. Facts are better than dreams.

Bill Deakin, the chief assistant in the team that compiled the war memoirs, once told Churchill's official biographer Martin Gilbert that Churchill's attitude to them was ' "this is not history, this is my case". He made it clear that it was his case he was making. It was an anthology – with his own papers – not a history.' That the work is an anthology and that it is team written, written by a group of hired collaborators which Churchill called the Syndicate, exempt it from the kind of literary comment which it has been possible to apply to Churchill's earlier writings. One member of the Syndicate, Dennis Kelly, a young barrister, remembered how he first participated in working over the several drafts and redactions which were then placed before the chief and titular author of the work. This was at Chartwell when Churchill was in his mid-seventies.

The first time I drafted a page of his war memoirs was a humbling and instructive experience. He had asked me to condense an expert's account of the German air attacks on London in the autumn and winter of 1940 – the Blitz. The expert's version ran to over one hundred and fifty pages and after ten days' effort I managed to reduce it to the three typewritten sheets he required. They seemed quite good till I sat beside him and he pulled out his red pen and slowly and patiently corrected what I had written. My sloppy, verbose sentences disappeared. Each paragraph was tightened and clarified, and their true meaning stood out.

It was like watching a skilful topiarist restoring a neglected and untidy garden-figure to its true shape and proportions. In the middle of this penitential process he gently turned to me and said: 'I hope you don't mind my doing this?' 'Sir,' I answered, 'I'm getting a free lesson in writing English.' He was visibly moved and from then on we worked in harness.

But such procedures whereby Churchill revised, edited and then assimilated to his personal story the reports of experts and the prose of the original documents were not effective in satisfying the expectations of his potential publishers. The criticisms made by Emery Reves were repeated, quite independently, by other readers, including the most important of the early bidders for the work, Henry Luce, who thought that the long documentary sections served to 'mar the architectural sense'. A vastly wealthy American publishing magnate, the proprietor of the Time-Life organisation, Henry Luce was to become a chief source of the massive sums of money that were paid to Churchill the writer during the late forties and the fifties. In November 1946 he offered Churchill well over a million dollars to serialise the memoirs in the United States. Houghton Mifflin would pay an extra quarter of a million dollars to publish the work as a book. As the memoirs grew, so did the size of Churchill's royalties. The writer who in the thirties had been embarrassingly in debt to the butcher and the grocer in Westerham now entered the years in which he was the writer as plutocrat. He ate well, he drank well, he travelled often and expensively, he bought farms near to Chartwell and he began a stable of racehorses with a quickly increasing number of jockeys and trainers in his pay. His writing now allowed him to buy all that he wished.

In the immediate postwar years restrictions on currency exchange were placed on British subjects and the limitations dramatically curtailed travel abroad. But Churchill with his huge income from America was not prevented from holidaying frequently in warm climates. On occasion the trips were gifts from his publishers. In January 1951, for example, Henry Luce and Time-Life financed a midwinter holiday for Churchill and also his large entourage of family members, friends and the Syndicate at Marrakesh, which Churchill had last visited at the time of that memorable meeting with Roosevelt. Walter Graebner, the London representative of Time-Life, worried about the expense and the tax implications of entertaining the cavalcade of guests accompanying the Leader of the Opposition. Mindful of the stern food rationing so recently in force in Britain, Graebner was struck by the great variety of food and drink available to Churchill and his numerous guests, the 'assortment of chicken breasts, cold roast beef and York hams, rolls and butter, rich cakes, fruit and several kinds of cheese. Champagne flowed copiously throughout the meal, and there was port for the cheese and brandy for the coffee.' When on such occasions Churchill was not actually painting he would entertain all his guests by 'singing old songs, telling slightly risqué stories and pressing drink ("It's *white* port, you know. All the ladies must have some because it's only *white* port") on everyone round him.' Also, as he had done with the Asquith party on the *Enchantress* all those years before, he would recite lines on simple pleasure from Thomas Gray's 'Ode To Spring'.

When Churchill decided to add an extra volume to his account of the Second World War, he had no hesitation in demanding another immediate advance from Henry Luce. 'You will I am sure not mind my saying that I certainly think in equity a further payment should be made by *Life* and the *New York Times* for the serialisation of Volume VI. This has undoubtedly proved a feature of first-rate importance to you . . .' But Churchill did pause to offer his thanks for his North African holiday. 'I must however repeat my thanks for the hospitality which you accorded me at Marrakesh and elsewhere in the currency difficulties from which we suffer so much in England.' In these same years Churchill worked hard for his publishers. It was a mark of his energy in his seventies that he was able to combine the duties of the leader of the parliamentary opposition with the demands of this remunerative but large and demanding literary enterprise. And in October of 1951, when he became Prime Minister for the second time, the work on his lengthy war memoirs was for the most part sketched out, though some writing needed to be done, chiefly by members of the Syndicate, before the final volume, *Triumph and Tragedy*, could appear in April 1954.

For Churchill the now eighty-year-old statesman this second period as Prime Minister was to be a time of endings and beginnings in world politics. It was a time that saw the death of Churchill's former political associate Joseph Stalin and the coming of new styles of communism in the Soviet Union; in the United States it saw the first Republican administration for twenty years, under the presidency of the D-day commander Dwight Eisenhower. In Britain there occurred the death of King George VI, with whom through all the anxieties of the war Churchill had developed a close friendship. In May 1953, at the time of the coronation of Queen Elizabeth II, British interests were being threatened in places as diverse as Malaya and the Canal Zone in Egypt. It was the time of involvement in the war in Korea and of French defeats in their colony of Indo-China. On Churchill's initiative Britain became armed with the hydrogen bomb.

For Churchill the writer this second Prime Ministership contained an occasion of world recognition. In October 1953 he learned that in Stockholm he had been awarded the Nobel Prize for Literature. When the ceremonies took place in Sweden in the following December, Churchill was represented by Clementine and by his daughter Mary. He himself was still on Bermuda, where he had attended a summit conference with his old friend President Eisenhower and the French prime minister, Joseph Laniel. They had discussed Korea, the proliferation of nuclear weapons, the course of the Cold War and relations with the now four-year-old communist regime in mainland China. Churchill was still suffering from the later effects of a major stroke. This had occurred at a formal dinner and reception at Downing Street, in honour of the Italian prime minister, less than three weeks after all the activities and excitement of the new Queen's coronation. Again Churchill's immense will power and resilience showed themselves as, within some four months, he recovered from a state of almost complete incapacity, to stand and address the Conservative party conference. But from this time on, the eighty-year-old Prime Minister became very aware of increasing pressure for him to resign and to allow himself to be replaced as Prime Minister by his long-time deputy and unchallenged successor, Anthony Eden. Churchill was slow and reluctant to let go power but in the middle of the decade, in early April 1955, he at last submitted his resignation to the Queen and his career as a wielder of political power came to an end, except for one last piece of advice tendered to the Queen in the following year.

But Churchill's career as a writer lasted longer. Around the time of the many national celebrations of his eightieth birthday he announced his commitment to a new literary project. He wrote a letter to his old friend Lord Hugh Cecil, the leader of the parliamentary Hughligans at the turn of the century, and told the now 85-year-old Linky (so called because he was thought in appearance to resemble the 'missing link' in the chain of evolution) that he had decided to resume work on what would be his *History of the English-Speaking Peoples*. He clearly regarded it as another big money-spinner, a new series of golden eggs. 'It will take four volumes. I lay one egg a year and will amuse myself with polishing and improving each in turn.' Within hours of leaving 10 Downing Street for the last time as Prime Minister Churchill, at home at Chartwell, began, as he approached his eighty-first year, to devote himself full-time to this last major work of prose.

The project in fact proved to be less a work of Churchill the writer than of Churchill the syndicate. Though one occasionally hears the unmistakable sound of the Churchill voice in the writing, it is not possible to regard him as, in any normal sense of the word, the author, the sentence-by-sentence organiser of the history. A new and leading figure in the syndicate that created this work was Alan Hodge, a friend of Brendan Bracken and a co-editor, together with Peter Quennell, of the monthly magazine *History Today*, which Bracken owned. Hodge's wife Jane remembered the long, complicated procedures whereby the Syndicate put these four volumes together, joining the reworked material Churchill had had written before the war with sections commissioned from historians at this later time. 'Immense drafts were turned in by J.H. Plumb and other historians and worked over by Churchill and Alan . . . with Churchill totally in command.' Many visitors to Chartwell at this time would be received by Churchill in his bedroom, which in his last years as a writer became his professional headquarters. There was a long tray-desk stretching across the bed with the long galley proofs of the *History* lying upon it. On the floor beside the bed, among all the straggling proofs, was a small aluminium pail for cigar ash. When Churchill's doctor Lord Moran was a visitor he also found the bed piled with history books such as Oman's *War in the Middle Ages*, J.R. Green's *The Last Plantaganets* and G.M. Trevelyan's *History of England*. Churchill told his doctor that 'when a difficult point arises I fatten my own account by referring to them'. Churchill told the Oxford historian A.L. Rowse that he was not satisfied with the sections of the history which he, Churchill, had written before the war. 'However, there were people who would read it on account of his "notoriety".'

Churchill's publishers, Cassell, assumed that there would indeed be a very large number of readers and purchasers of this work of compilation. When it was published on 23 April, St George's Day, 1956, it had a print run of 130,000 copies. Within a month, 30,000 more were printed. Churchill's income went up accordingly. But he still laboured away at the later volumes. A good deal of the work on these was done at La Pausa, the home on the French Riviera of his agent Emery Reves and Emery's wife-to-be Wendy Russell. When first a guest there Churchill wrote uneasily about his host's unwedded state to Clementine, who had strict views about such matters. But when Emery married Wendy Russell, Churchill felt more comfortable there and visited and worked at La Pausa regularly and for increasingly long periods. 'My hosts are very artistic,' Winston wrote to Clementine; 'they paint and they collect. More than that they delight in the famous painters of Europe & I am having an education in art . . . Also they play Mozart & others on these multiplied gramophones.' On one of his visits to La Pausa to write, Churchill met Aristole Onassis, the wealthy Greek shipping magnate, who admired him greatly and later entertained him on many occasions on his yacht. Robert Boothby once recalled, in this connection, a cameo scene after lunch on the Côte d'Azur. As the octogenarian Churchill dropped off to sleep a wealthy lady, Mrs Daisy Fellows, the Singer sewing machine heiress, remarked 'What a pity that so great a man should end his life in the company of Onassis and Wendy Reves.' To their horror Churchill opened one eye and said: 'Daisy, Wendy Reves is something you will never be. She is young, she is beautiful and she is kind.' Then the eye closed again.

In October 1956, as Churchill's successor Anthony Eden grappled unsuccessfully with the Suez Crisis, Churchill continued to exchange very warm letters with his agent's wife, signing himself 'with much love' and planning to return as soon as possible to La Pausa, or Pausaland, as he had come to call it. Shortly after serving as one of the advisers who recommended to the Queen that Harold Macmillan should be invited to take the place of the ailing Anthony Eden as Prime Minister, Churchill and his entourage returned to La Pausa, where he enjoyed the same adulation, the same unstinting attention to his every comfort that Wendy Reves had so enjoyed giving him on all his previous visits. But on this occasion Clementine joined the party and Wendy was greatly hurt by Lady Churchill's attitude to her. On his return to Britain Churchill tried to soothe his young hostess, writing, 'Clemmie was astonished that you thought her manner to you had hardened. Do put it out of your mind, my dear. With all my love and best wishes - - -W'

Clementine did not return to the Reves home for some considerable time, but Churchill continued to holiday and to write there. He took a close interest in his hosts, noting on one of his arrivals, 'Wendy is very well and has put on weight without impairing her figure in any way.' Clementine had misgivings about the situation at La Pausa and she let them be known to Churchill's bodyguard, Detective Sergeant Murray. 'Lady Churchill is rather worried by the amount that gets into the Press when Sir Winston is at La Pausa – false rumours about his health today, and in the past details of his day-to-day life. You know the sort of thing I mean.' In February 1958 Churchill came down with bronchial pneumonia at La Pausa but he recovered and in the following year Wendy sent him her greetings on his eighty-fifth birthday; 'Tomorrow is your birthday, dear . . . I cannot believe that you will be eighty-five. So young in heart you are to me.'

But within a year this friendship ran into painful difficulties when the Reveses felt that they could not agree to Churchill's latest request to return to La Pausa. In a long letter to his distinguished client Reves wrote about 'the intrigues' which certain people had engaged in to destroy the Reveses' friendship with Churchill. Wendy had been made ill by it all. 'There is a certain way', her husband wrote, 'of disregarding other people's feelings which drives a sensitive human being to the border of insanity.' Deeply saddened, the 85-year-old Churchill accepted the ending of this close friendship and wrote to Wendy thanking her for all that she had done for him. 'I am sorry to hear that you were vexed with me, and I cannot allow you to leave for America without telling you that the months I spent at your charming house were among the brightest in my life, and I shall always think of them as such.'

The professional relationship between Churchill and Emery Reves, that between author and agent, remained an important part of Churchill's life as a writer. One memorable occasion occurred when Reves was able to submit to Churchill what he believed to be, at that time, 'the highest amount ever paid for a manuscript'. This was

£20,000 for a 10,000-word epilogue to an abridged version of the war memoirs which the publishers thought it advisable to bring out. This proved to be Churchill's last literary commission. Only in 1963, less than two years before his death at the age of ninety, would Churchill, with great reluctance, retire as a Member of Parliament. But six years earlier he explicitly acknowledged the conclusion of his career as a writer. To his old friend and financial adviser Bernard Baruch, the Wall Street speculator and Democratic party adviser, Churchill wrote, saying quite simply, 'I have now retired from literature and am endeavouring to find ways of spending pleasantly the remaining years of my life.'

This marked the conclusion of a career in letters which had lasted for just about sixty years. It was a career that had ended in spectacular financial successes. But the highly remunerated works of the last third of Churchill's writing career, the hundreds and hundreds of pages that make up the history of the Second World War and the English-speaking peoples, are not what constitute Winston Churchill's literary achievement. These books made him a fortune; earlier books made him a place in English literary history. The vivid and compelling narrative line of the young war correspondent in *The River War*, the keen close sympathy of the biographer of Lord Randolph Churchill and of the first Duke of Marlborough, these are some of the qualities that make Churchill's writing live for us still. His special gifts with the language in the earlier works are enough to protect his overall literary achievement from charges of empty rhetorical phrasing, the compulsive but often meaningless grand manner and the recurrence of large abstract nouns which are, at best, remote from experience and, at their worst, just verbiage. Churchill as a major prose writer is often best seen in the smaller, more modest prose forms, in his essays and character portraits. Here his special abilities with words most clearly show themselves, his delicately insinuating humour, his sense of drama, his fine ironies, his generous understanding, his humanity. If literary criticism must concede his overall *oeuvre* to be uneven, it must also declare that these qualities serve to rank a good part of it with the major discursive prose in the canon of English literature in this century.

Index

Note: titles in **bold** refer to Churchill's writings.

L32a